DRESS FITTING

Also available from Blackwell Science

Dress Pattern Designing
The Basic Principles of Cut and Fit
Fifth Edition
Natalie Bray
With Fashion Supplement by Ann Haggar
0 632 01881 X

More Dress Pattern Designing
Fourth Edition
Natalie Bray
With Fashion Supplement by Ann Haggar
0 632 01883 6

Metric Pattern Cutting
Third Edition
Winifred Aldrich
0 632 03612 5

Metric Pattern Cutting for Menswear
Including Computer Aided Design
Third Edition
Winifred Aldrich
0 632 04113 7

Metric Pattern Cutting for Children's Wear
Second Edition
Winifred Aldrich
0 632 03057 7

Pattern Grading for Women's Clothes
The Technology of Sizing
Gerry Cooklin
0 632 02295 7

Pattern Grading for Men's Cltohes
The Technology of Sizing
Gerry Cooklin
0 632 03305 3

Pattern Grading for Children's Clothes
The Technology of Sizing
Gerry Cooklin
0 632 02612 X

Modelling on the Dress Stand
Janice Mee and Michael Purdy
0 632 01884 4

Pattern Cutting for Women's Outerwear
Gerry Cooklin
0 632 03797 0

Pattern Cutting for Lingerie, Beachwear and
Leisurewear
Ann Haggar
0 632 02033 4

Fashion Source Book
Edited by Kathryn McKelvie
0 632 03993 0

Illustrating Fashion
Kathryn McKelvie and Janine Munslow
0 632 04024 6

DRESS FITTING

Basic Principles and Practice

NATALIE BRAY

Former Principal of
The Katinka School of Dress Designing, London

Illustrations by Wanda and Tadeusz Orlowicz

b

Blackwell
Science

© Natalie Bray 1970, 1978

Blackwell Science Ltd
Editorial Offices:
Osney Mead, Oxford OX2 0EL
25 John Street, London WC1N 2PL
23 Ainslie Place, Edinburgh EH3 6AJ
350 Main Street, Malden
  MA 02148 5018, USA
54 University Street, Carlton
  Victoria 3053, Australia

Other Editorial Offices:
Arnette Blackwell SA
  224, Boulevard Saint Germain
  75007 Paris, France

Blackwell Wissenschafts-Verlag GmbH
  Kurfürstendamm 57
  10707 Berlin, Germany

  Zehetnergasse 6
  A-1140 Wien
  Austria

First published in Great Britain by
  Crosby Lockwood & Son Ltd 1970
Reprinted by Granada Publishing Limited
  in Crosby Lockwood Staples 1973
Second edition (metric) published 1978
Reprinted 1978, 1979 (ISBN 0 258 97095 2)
Reissued in paperback by
  Granada Publishing Ltd 1982
Reprinted 1984 (ISBN 0 246 11849 0)
Reprinted by BSP Professional Books
  1987, 1991
Reprinted by Blackwell Science Ltd
  1994, 1997

Printed and bound in Great Britain at
the Alden Press Limited, Oxford and Northampton

The Blackwell Science logo is a trade mark of
Blackwell Science Ltd, registered at the
United Kingdom Trade Marks Registry

DISTRIBUTORS

Marston Book Services Ltd
PO Box 269
Abingdon
Oxon OX14 4YN
(*Orders*: Tel: 01235 465500
          Fax: 01235 465555)

USA
  Blackwell Science, Inc.
  Commerce Place
  350 Main Street
  Malden, MA 021428 5018
  (*Orders*: Tel: 800 759-6102
                  617 388-8250
            Fax: 617 388-8255)

Canada
  Copp Clark Professional
  200 Adelaide Street, West, 3rd Floor
  Toronto, Ontario M5H 1W7
  (*Orders*: Tel: 416 597-1616
                  800 815-9417
            Fax: 416 597-1617)

Australia
  Blackwell Science Pty Ltd
  54 University Street
  Carlton, Victoria 3053
  (*Orders*: Tel: 03 9347-0300
            Fax: 03 9347-5001)

A catalogue record for this title
is available from the British Library

ISBN 0-632-01879-8

CONTENTS

INTRODUCTORY

This book is based on a set of Fitting Notes which were originally used in connection with a course of lessons given at the Katinka School of Dress Designing.

Since, in the past, the Notes were accompanied by practical demonstrations and verbal explanations, in the absence of these it became necessary for publication purposes to expand the Notes with additional exercises and to illustrate them with many diagrams and sketches, so as to make them more self-explanatory.

The subject of Fitting can be approached in several different ways. It can be dealt with very simply by just giving some general advice and elementary rules without explaining or analyzing any of the 'fitting problems'. Such simple instructions must of necessity be brief and of a very general nature. Dealing usually with a random selection of faults, they may not apply to the particular case in hand, and seldom, if ever, help *to build up reliable fitting experience*. The subject of Fitting can also be treated more fundamentally as one involving an anatomical study of the figure and a detailed survey of all its irregularities. This is a perfectly logical approach, but the considerable amount of theoretical study required before any application to practical fitting can be introduced makes it unduly long and cumbersome. In this book a middle course has been adopted, combining theoretical explanations with their direct application to the various problems which face a fitter.

To be able *to understand* what is happening when observing a defect is already to have an idea of how to correct it. Learning how to fit is a step-by-step process of building up a store of **basic knowledge with practical experience**: every learner must go through it before acquiring the ability, not just *to see* a defect, but to assess it correctly as a *fitting problem* created by the shape of the figure, and so to choose with ever increasing confidence the right method·of dealing with it.

It is obvious, therefore, that fitting experience can be developed constructively only in connection with a knowledge of pattern cutting: otherwise there is nothing to which one can refer the various practical observations one is accumulating. A defect is, after all, a mistake in the construction of the pattern, due, it is true, to an irregularity in the shape of the figure and not necessarily to a badly cut pattern, but a mistake all the same. It must be put right *as if adjusting a pattern*.

A particular difficulty in discussing the subject of fitting is the choice of a suitable plan for the presentation of the various fitting problems. A simple list of defects is of little practical value because of the difficulty of identifying defects and still more of *describing them* with any degree of accuracy: there are many creases, big and small, which on the surface look very similar but are in fact the result of different causes and so require different treatment. All this makes a simple enumeration of defects and corrections quite unreliable in practice, just as it makes even the compiling of a simple Index very difficult, if not impossible.

Defects are connected with, and conditioned by, a variety of circumstances: shape of figure, type of garment and the way it is worn, the texture of the fabric, etc.—all this can affect the fit of a garment. This interconnection of everything complicates, of course, the general fitting situation by making it difficult to isolate a defect in order to examine it 'in vacuum' as it were; but on the other hand it also helps by making it easier *to identify defects through their connection*—mainly with types of figure—and so to understand their cause. Observing, for instance, a certain shape of figure such as a stooping one, a fitter already *expects* certain defects usually associated with the type of figure, and so is more prepared to deal with them: this of course adds considerably to a fitter's confidence. Considering defects *in their relation to* shapes of figure, to posture, to various 'fashion lines' and even to some styles and fabrics, contributes much to the building up of that valuable practical experience which every good fitter possesses.

It is always difficult *to describe* defects in garments, and one tends to mention more symptoms than there may actually be in an individual case. It is also difficult *to illustrate* them for the same reason: not all the drags and creases mentioned or shown in the diagrams will necessarily be there in every example. Drawings, on the whole, have to be made 'diagrammatic' to exclude details irrelevant to the particular point under discussion. This is a difficulty sometimes experienced with photographs, where it is often impossible to eliminate *unnecessary* details.

Finally, one must consider the question of the **standard of fit**, which has been much influenced by the wholesale manufacturing trade. It is perfectly understandable that one does not expect a bought dress or suit to fit as well in every detail as one made to measure and, as a result of this, some defects are no longer regarded as such, or are accepted as unavoidable, or are simply ignored. On the whole ready-to-wear clothes do fit a very great number of people, even though often more by virtue of their style and cut than correct size and proportions. Elegant cut and style and general attractiveness of fabric and trimmings is very much the secret of the ready-to-wear garment; and so women easily accept a few or even many creases and often a wrong size, e.g. one that is too tight, because the general effect on the figure is pleasing. On the other hand, it is a well known fact that clothes made to individual measurements sometimes miss this effect for various reasons: the style may turn out to be unbecoming, or too much 'chopping and changing' by the customer at fittings may spoil the 'line' of the design, or the garment may be overfitted, i.e. made to follow the figure too closely instead of 'concealing' it, or for some other reason. The most careful fitting is no absolute guarantee of final success, which depends on many factors, some of them purely psychological.

Nevertheless, there are many figures for whom a fitting is a definite advantage and even essential, even though the standard of fit expected may vary. Because of the variety of possible defects—from simple 'wrong size' to quite complicated style adjustments—a book on Fitting must consider systematically as wide a range of problems as possible, leaving the final decision—to correct or not to correct—to the judgement of the fitter.

Out of the eight chapters of this book, two chapters are not directly concerned with fitting adjustments as such. Chapter One, dealing with Modelling, provides in a practical form much of the *background knowledge* on which fitting skill is based. Chapter Eight considers the question of adapting an *average* block pattern to *individual measurements*—a subject which connects itself quite naturally with the whole problem of achieving a good fit.

As the subject dealt with in this book involves little, if any, *precise* measuring, and contains no drafting which depends for good results on definite figures and proportions, the conversion of imperial measurements into metric in this edition is not a precise conversion to the nearest millimetre of every figure mentioned in the original edition.

In Fitting, as in the case of style interpretation and pattern designing, a freer approach to metrication is not only possible, but desirable. Since, by its very nature, Fitting cannot be a precise technique and is always to a certain extent experimental, any figures used must of necessity be approximate and thus, in metricating this book, it has been found possible to make wide use of the conventional interpretation of various frequently used figures and measurements such as the use of 1 cm for $\frac{1}{2}''$ and 0·5 cm for $\frac{1}{4}''$. In a few cases, however it has been found necessary to make use of the plus and minus signs, which indicate that it is essential, in the given instance, to measure more precisely, i.e. 2–3 mm more or less than the whole centimetre.

To assist the Fitter, the Table of Average Measurements and Proportions originally given in the *metric edition* of 'Dress Pattern Designing', is reprinted here at end of chapter 8. This Table can be of considerable help not only in guiding the drafting of new blocks, or as a general reference chart for checking and comparing results, but also in taking individual measurements more correctly. As accurate measuring of the figure is always difficult and results tend to vary from one measurer to another, even when the same or a similar system of measuring is used, a table covering a range of average sizes is very useful as it immediately shows up a measurement which is too far removed from the average, and either makes one check it again, or, if confirmed, draws special attention to it as a possible fitting problem. All this applies even more to metric measurements as here the measuring unit is so much smaller that it is extremely easy to pull in the tape measure to register 1 cm more or less, with the result that measurements can become very approximate unless a reliable check by *standard proportions* can be applied at the same time. The reader will also find it useful to refer to this Table while studying Chapter Eight.

CHAPTER ONE | PRELIMINARY MODELLING EXERCISES

The object of these exercises is to show how the fabric behaves when applied in different ways to the curves and hollows of the figure, and to demonstrate the many possibilities of manipulating it to achieve certain effects of line and fit.

However general and theoretical these exercises may appear, they are closely connected with many of the problems encountered by a fitter. In fact, the results obtained through these exercises can be said to represent much of the practical knowledge normally acquired slowly over years of cutting and fitting experience.

This background knowledge, which is at the command of every experienced fitter, is obtained quite naturally in the course of practical work by method of trial and error, through correct or incorrect analysis of defects, and through various deductions made from fitting mistakes.

The few simple modelling exercises introduced here aim at speeding up this slow experimental way of acquiring fitting skill. They bring directly to the notice of the student certain essential basic facts which every fitter sooner or later must understand and learn to appreciate if this skill is to be based on something more substantial than a so-called 'common sense approach' or haphazard coping with difficulties.

These exercises demonstrate why certain results will always be obtained when the fabric is handled and applied to the figure in a certain way. Modelling is an excellent fitting instructor, and working on the stand is the quickest way of understanding the basic factors which underlie various fitting problems.

In all cases an average stand, Bust 88 cm or 92 cm is used, but the exercises could be carried out on almost any size of stand provided it is reasonably modern in shape, i.e. with a well curved bustline, not too big a waist, and with some curve of the back in the shoulder and neck part. It is difficult to observe some of the results described in these exercises if the stand has not sufficient curve, i.e. if it is too flat in the back or front, or has a thick waist and neck. In any case, even with a well shaped stand, padding will occasionally be recommended in order to obtain a more correct effect of a faulty figure posture or other defect, such as a prominent shoulder blade, extra high bust, etc. Such pads are easily made by folding or crumpling bits of material or leno, or even paper (tissue paper) without attempting to finish them off in any way. They are merely pinned to the stand where necessary. In most cases, however, it will be sufficient to use one's imagination in *visualizing an unusual shape of figure*.

For the actual modelling several kinds of material, such as fairly heavy mull, *soft* calico, or leno (tarlatan) can be used. Of these leno is particularly suitable for such exercises (even if sometimes too fragile for actual patterns), not only because of its crisp texture and easy handling, but mainly because of *clearly visible grain*: it is always easy to refer to the grain and to follow it accurately in leno. To be able to note the various changes in the position of the straight grain (SG), whether lengthwise (L–SG) or crosswise (X–SG), is most instructive and necessary when studying the fundamentals of correct fit.

It is of course possible to invent many such exercises, but restriction of space makes it necessary to keep to a basic selection which, it is hoped, will be sufficiently wide in its range *to make the fitting problems dealt with in subsequent chapters more intelligible*. Students of fitting are, however, advised to learn *to experiment on the stand* in a similar way whenever any real problem of cut or fit presents itself in the course of their work.

The first six exercises, dealing with the back of a bodice, introduce some of the fundamental principles which must sooner or later be understood by every fitter, and which help to explain many of the fitting troubles connected with the shape of the back and the fitting of the waist. The remaining six refer to the front, without necessarily following the same order, but rather underlining that which it is particularly important to understand and bear in mind when fitting the front of a bodice. In both groups fitting defects are not actually dealt with but just mentioned, for a more detailed discussion of these belongs to the next chapter.

Chapter One deals only with the modelling of the bodice; some modelling of collars and skirts is introduced in later chapters.

1

EXERCISE I—WAIST-LENGTH BACK FITTED TO THE FIGURE
The surplus fullness of the back

Use a rectangle of leno 52 cm long (i.e. CB length to waist plus 10–12 cm) and 28–30 cm wide. Pin the selvedge, or L–SG edge folded back 1 cm, to the stand at the CB nape and waist, leaving 5 cm above the nape (Fig. 1). A *temporary* pin can be used in the region of the shoulder blade to keep the leno in position while modelling.

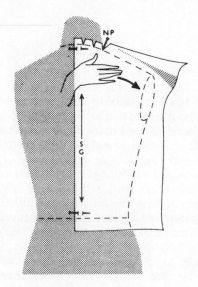

FIG. 1/I

Begin by **cutting the neckline**, allowing a 1 cm turning and snipping into it while smoothing the leno *away from the CB* towards the shoulder. Keep the *neckline quite flat* and use a pin at the Neck Point (NP). After smoothing the leno along the shoulder towards the armhole, fold it back along the middle of the shoulder and cut with a 2 cm turning. Since the shoulder is kept quite flat, **some fullness will come down into the armhole**. Pin at the Shoulder Point (SP), just stabbing the pin into the stand.

Going over to the waist (Fig. 2), smooth the leno *away from* the CB and slightly up. Working step by step, and applying the leno well to the stand, cut just below the waist, i.e. leaving a 2 cm turning. Apply the leno carefully to the waist after each cut. Snip the turning where necessary, so that **no fullness remains in the waist.**

It will be observed that the crosswise straight grain (X–SG) does not follow the waistline, but *tends to go up*: forcing it down to waist level would leave some fullness or ease in the waist. The fabric must be allowed to lie naturally and this will bring the side waist point (W) a little *below* the SG level of the CB waist (see detail *a*). The bigger the waist hollow (and even stands may vary in this respect), the bigger the difference between the two levels will be.

Near the side continue to smooth the leno, but now slightly *up towards the armhole* (to keep the waist quite tight). Pin at UP. For the side seam fold back the leno in a straight, i.e. *vertical* line; cut, leaving a 2 cm turning and pin to the stand. It will be found that some surplus fullness has been pushed into the armhole where it joins the small amount from the top (Fig. 3). Cut the *loose armhole* roughly to shape.

Check the fit of the whole back: it must be kept *as flat*

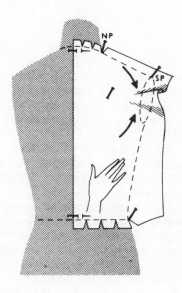

FIG. 2/I

and smooth as possible, concentrating all the floating surplus fullness of the back in the armhole where it should be clearly visible, even on a stand. On a figure, *with more curve of shoulder blade and waist*, this fullness may be much more pronounced. **It is one of the main fitting problems of the back.**

It is quite obvious that the fullness cannot be left in this position. **The back armhole should be kept quite flat,** and so, since this fullness cannot be 'darted' here, it must be dealt with somehow *before* it reaches the armhole: it must, in fact, be *distributed* to other parts of the pattern.

The exercise thus demonstrates that: *a*) surplus back fullness does exist and that it may be more or less pronounced according to the posture of the figure and shape (or curve) of the back (see Fig. 4 lower); *b*) if it is ignored, it may get into the armhole where even a small amount results in unsightly creases and may interfere with sleeve fitting; *c*) it must be dealt with *before it reaches the armhole* because, once there, it is not easy to get rid of it *at the fitting* (easing on a tape, shrinking or padding are

EXERCISE II—WAIST-LENGTH BACK SHAPED
BY DARTS
Correct distribution of the surplus back fullness

Use a similar piece of material and pin it at the nape, as before. At the waist level, before pinning, first snip into the selvedge and fold back 2 cm, as shown in Fig. 5. The fold may run off to nothing at the nape (when there is no CB seam) or be dealt with as explained later in Exercise IV.

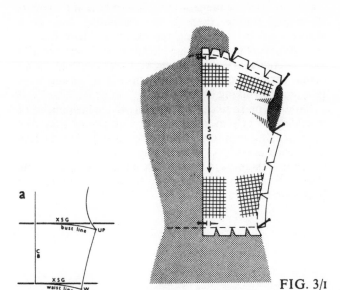

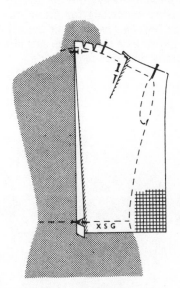

FIG. 3/1

FIG. 5/1

but additional emergency corrections). The exercise shows, in fact, that it is **impossible to mould a flat piece of fabric to the back** without having to contend with some **surplus fullness**, unless the back is exceptionally flat which it seldom, if ever, is in a modern figure.

To verify the statement that **a more protruding shoulder blade would make it all worse**, pin a pad of leno or paper to the stand (detail) in the right position to represent a higher shoulder blade, and model over it (Fig. 4). It will be found that the side seam has to be pushed up more than before, to avoid diagonal drags from the shoulder blade, that the *armhole becomes looser*, and that there is more fullness to deal with.

Exercise II shows how to deal with this basic problem of surplus fullness.

When modelling the neckline keep it slightly eased and not smoothed towards the shoulder, as was done in Exercise I. The same applies to the shoulder seam which has a small shoulderblade dart half-way down its length, taking out 1–2 cm *to prevent any fullness from being pushed into the armhole*. The actual method of dealing with **the fullness in the top part of a bodice** may vary, e.g. it can be used in small darts (even tucks) in the neckline (detail *a*) or at NP (detail *b*), or just *eased* a little into neckline and front shoulder (detail *c*). Surplus fullness can also be made to disappear in a seam, i.e. a Panel seam (detail *d*).

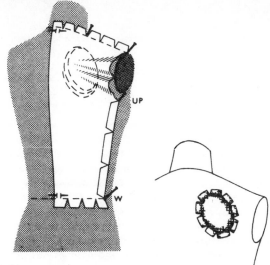

FIG. 4/1

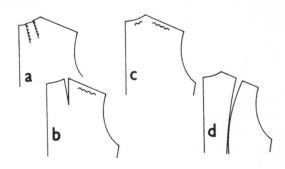

At the waist the surplus fullness has already been reduced by the *slanting of the* CB. Proceed to model along the waistline where some of the fullness will now be taken out in **a waist dart** below the shoulder blade (Fig. 6). For an average figure this is usually a 2–2·5 cm, dart. Begin by measuring 9 cm (¼ of Back width) from CB and here crease the leno along the L–SG, the crease to be the middle of the dart (detail). Pin the dart 13–15 cm up, using several pins. **N.B.** The dart here is shown *folded outside* and standing away from the pattern: this is more convenient when modelling for *fitting* purposes. Darts can, however, be *folded inside*, to lie quite flat, with just a line (seam) showing on the surface, as if already stitched. This is generally preferred in designing.

If, after all these precautions, the armhole still appears loose and untidy, there is the possibility (though a limited one) of smoothing the excess armhole fullness up and increasing the shoulderblade dart. There are also various emergency adjustments which may be made on an actual garment, e.g. tightening armhole by easing it on to a tape, shrinking or padding.

Padding of shoulders, if permitted by fashion, is of considerable help in fitting as it is a quick and easy way of remedying armhole defects and so reducing darting and easing elsewhere. That is why, when padding is out of fashion, there is more insistence on using clearly visible shoulderblade darts—the chief means of making the back armhole neat.

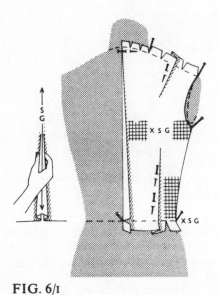

FIG. 6/I

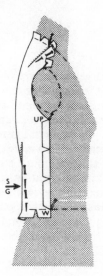

FIG. 7/I

Cut the back 2 cm below the waist, snipping the turning where necessary to keep the leno quite smooth. Complete the side seam in a straight (vertical) line (Fig. 7). Note that the X–SG now follows the waistline and to obtain a flat waist fit it will not be necessary to smooth the leno upwards, as in the first exercise. This is **the effect of the waist dart**. Seam is slightly 'off the grain'.

N.B. A bigger waist dart can be used instead of the slanted CB, which is of course a *concealed* dart.

The **surplus fullness** of the back has thus been **distributed between several points** where it is either invisibly suppressed (by easing) or taken out in darts. This is the way it is usually dealt with in a modern pattern which must always make allowance for some curve in the shape of the back.

EXERCISE III—WAIST-LENGTH BACK EXTENDED BY HIP YOKE
Long shaped bodice with a waist join

Using the back already modelled in Exercise II, add **a hip yoke** to it. Place a 30 cm square of leno with the selvedge to the CB in such a way that 1–2 cm is folded back at the waist *to match the top part*, the fold running off to nothing at hip level 22 cm below the waist (Fig. 8). Pin at the waist and hips, leaving 2·5 cm above, cut along the waist, applying the leno well to the stand, and taking out a waist dart corresponding in depth and position to the waist dart in the top part of the bodice. Pin this dart 15–17 cm down and then continue cutting and modelling until the side is reached.

After pinning the waist dart, it will be noted that the top edge of the leno beyond the dart swings a little up towards the side and the final waist point (W), when later seen on the flat, comes above the horizontal level of the waist (detail *a*) because the waist now is slightly curved. In fact, if the yoke pattern were placed on the table below the top part, waistlines touching—*both parts with their waist darts pinned*—the two side waist points *W would overlap* (Fig. 9). This is an important thing to note as it shows how, with a closer fit to the figure, *extra underarm length* seems to appear *at the side waist* (W) just where needed to provide for the waist hollow.

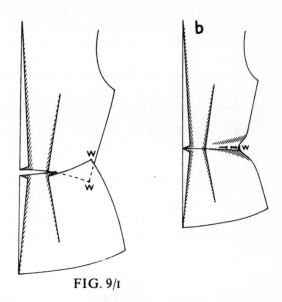

FIG. 9/ɪ

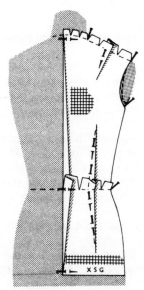

FIG. 8/ɪ

N.B. If the darts of the yoke are unpinned, the shape of the *flat pattern* will be found to be quite different, and, provided the waist darts of the top part are also not used there will be little or no overlap at W points. This once again confirms that the side seam fluting at the waist is definitely connected with a closer fit of the back.

Returning to the stand, pin the *trimmed top edge* of the yoke (which now has no turning) over the turning of the top part of the bodice so that they are joined into **a complete shaped back**. Cut the lower edge of the yoke 22 cm below the waist to a straight line parallel to the lower edge of the stand.

If the whole pinned pattern is now removed from the stand and, *with the waist still joined*, laid on the table (detail *b*) with the CB to an almost straight line, it will be seen that there is 'fluting' at the side waist due to the overlapping of points W (seen in Fig. 9). It is not difficult to understand that this apparent extra side length is caused by *the closer fit* of this long back.

A hip yoke can also be modelled **without waist darts** by moulding the leno well to the figure (Fig. 10). Such a yoke will have the same *shape* (though not the same grain) as the darted yoke, *so long as the darts of the latter remain pinned* (detail *c*). When placed below a close fitting back it will overlap at the side points (W) in the same way as in Fig. 9.

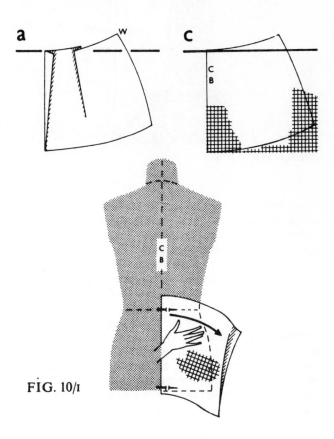

FIG. 10/ɪ

EXERCISE IV—HIP-LENGTH BACK: TIGHT OR SEMI-SHAPED
Long tight bodice without a waist join

The backs of two hip-length bodices are demonstrated here:

   A—Back without waist darts but with a CB seam

   B—Back with waist darts and with or without a CB seam

A—The first version has no waist darts and all the shaping for a tight or semi-shaped fit is achieved only by a CB seam and the two side seams.

Take a rectangle of leno about 70 cm long and 30 cm wide and, leaving 5 cm above, pin it to the CB at the nape, the waist and the hips. At the waist, before pinning, snip into the selvedge, and fold it back 2 cm, as in Exercise II. Run the fold off to nothing at the top 10 cm below the

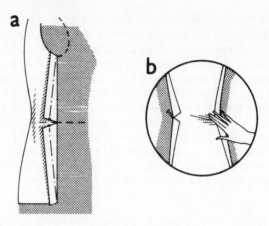

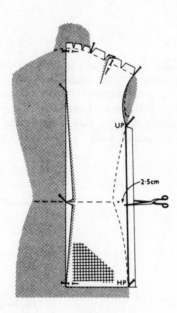

FIG. 11/I

nape (pin), and at the bottom 22 cm below the waist, i.e. on the hip level (Fig. 11). The CB line now follows the curve of the spine and *must have a seam*: it cannot be placed to the fold of the material.

Model the top part of the bodice following Exercise II, with a dart on the shoulder and a neat armhole. Pin at NP, SP and UP: the latter is placed in the middle of the underarm (22–23 cm from CB in this size).

On the hip level apply the leno straight across (X–SG horizontal) and mark HP *in line with UP* (HP is usually just over 1 cm farther out from CB than UP). Fold the leno back between UP and HP in a vertical line and cut with a small turning in preparation for the shaping, i.e. the *curving* of the side seam. For a closer fit this straight line will have to go in at least 2·5 cm and through this

point the side seam will be curved (detail *a*). This is still a provisional seam.

When applying the curved side seam to the hollow of the figure it will be observed that **the seam feels tight at the waist**, i.e. it does not cling to the side, and if pressed well into it, i.e. fitted tighter, produces creases at the waist (detail *b*).

Further curving-in of the seam, therefore, even though later possibly necessary for a close fit, will not *by itself* release the tension at the side waist sufficiently, nor eliminate the waist creases: **the side seam needs lengthening** just where it is tight, i.e. **in the hollow of the waist**, not at UP or HP.

To prove this, cut from the side into the waist, about half-way to CB or more: this releases the tightness and, as a gap opens at the seam, *the leno can be applied closer to the figure* (Fig. 12). Secure the gap by inserting into it

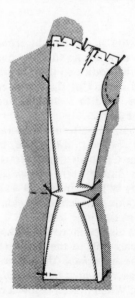

FIG. 12/I

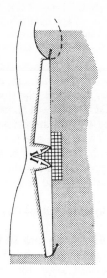

FIG. 13/I

a small piece of leno. Note that the closer the leno is applied to the figure, i.e. the tighter the fit, the bigger the gap will be.

The *final side seam* (Fig. 13) can now be *shaped over the gap* by drawing the line of the seam to appear straight when viewed from the side. This automatically gives the correct amount of curving for the side seam (about 4 cm or more in from the original straight seam). For a less tight fit at the waist, such as would be required for **a semi-shaped bodice**, the gap should open out less and the seam curve will be smaller. The tightness and waist curving of the side seam will thus vary according to the closeness of fit required, and also according to whether any additional means of shaping the waist, e.g. waist darts, are used or not (see version B).

The exercise shows that for a good waist fit of **a long tight bodice without a waist join or waist darts**, the **tightness of the side seam** may present a real fitting problem. This can only be solved according to the details of the style, the texture of the fabric and the shape of the figure, i.e. when all these circumstances are favourable: a figure with a hollow back waist, for instance, or the use of a very stiff fabric will always make the problem much more difficult.

As was seen in Exercise III, a back with a waist join provides the extra length required at the side waist quite naturally through 'overlapping' of the waist points W (see Fig. 9). Since, in a dress without a waist join, one obviously cannot cut into the waist (as was done in this exercise), the side of a *dartless* fitted bodice can be lengthened only by stretching. Because of this, the plain close fitting back presents the biggest problem in waist fitting, particularly when—as often happens—it has no CB seam (CB is to the fold), and when, moreover, it is cut in **a fabric which resists stretching**.

Normally, a certain amount of stretching occurs with most *curved* side seams in the course of making up and pressing, if the fabric is soft and of a reasonably stretchy texture (soft woollen, silk, velvet, chiffon, lace, etc.): here ordinary pressing disposes of the problem of waist creases fairly easily. A fitter will allow for this and not worry about *a few* creases at the fitting if the seam can be relied upon to 'give' sufficiently later. A fitter may also rely to a certain extent on the weight of the skirt (e.g. a long, full skirt) to pull the bodice *down* into better shape and so smooth out the fit of the waist.

On the whole, this type of back, particularly without a CB seam, is *more suitable for a semi-shaped style* which is not expected to be quite so close fitting, and in which some waist creasing is usually quite acceptable.

B—The second version has waist darts and is cut either with a CB seam, i.e. shaped to the CB, or without one, when it can be placed to the fold of the material.

For a **bodice with a CB seam**, model as in the previous exercise. After pinning the CB, complete the top as far as UP.

Take out a waist dart 9 cm from CB. At this distance first crease the material lengthwise up and down, following L–SG; then measure and pin out the depth of the dart at the waist, 2·5–4 cm or according to the size of the waist. Complete the dart tapering it off to nothing 14 cm up and 16 cm down from the waist (Fig. 14). Use several pins and snip the dart at the waist. The dart will naturally be deeper if no CB seam is used.

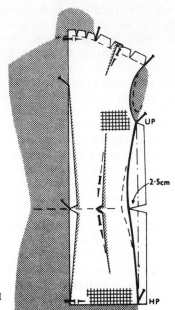

FIG. 14/I

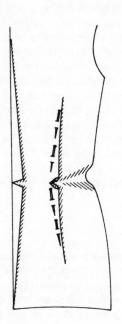

FIG. 15/1

EXERCISE V—MOVING THE SURPLUS BACK FULLNESS
A—moving the fullness down
B—moving the fullness up

In the first exercise it was demonstrated that the back of a bodice has some surplus fullness, caused by the curves of the figure, i.e. of the spine, the shoulder blade and the hollow of the waist. Exercise II showed how this fullness should be distributed and suppressed at several points to avoid concentrating it in one place where it might be difficult to deal with. It will now be shown how it can be moved from one position to another and what effect this has on the 'silhouette' of the bodice or dress.

A—Surplus fullness moved into the hem (at waist or hip level).
Using a longer (63–68 cm) and wider (38 cm) piece of leno, pin it to CB at the nape and about 15 cm *below the waist*, keeping it taut over the waist hollow. Begin modelling as usual but, instead of making a dart on the shoulder, smooth the leno *down into the armhole* and from there *down into the underarm seam*. Note that at this stage the leno, which is quite flat at the top, begins to stand away from the figure in the lower part (Fig. 16).

For **the side seam** fold leno back in a vertical line from UP and note that it will be off the grain, i.e. *sloping out* from SG. The lower edge, whether at waist level or hip level, stands away from the figure; the **surplus fullness is now in the hem** (detail *a*). N.B. This effect shows more clearly if a *whole back*, i.e. a double piece of leno is modelled on both sides of the stand.

On the hip line bring the leno over to the side and mark HP in line with UP. Fold leno back between UP and HP in a straight line and cut with a small turning. Snip in 2·5 cm at the waist and *curve the side seam through this point*. (Fig. 14). On applying the seam to the waist hollow it will be found that it is easier to do so than in the first case and there is usually only a slight tightness (if any), in spite of the comparatively small curve of the side seam. The reason for this is that the taking out of the waist dart pulls the side seam in towards the CB, and produces a kind of 'flare' at the waist (Fig. 15). This actually introduces some extra length where needed, i.e. in the hollow of the waist, so that no further lengthening (stretching at W) is required except perhaps for a very tight fit.

All this can be proved if the pattern, *with the waist darts still pinned* and the CB kept to a straight or *almost straight* line (Fig. 15) is laid on the table: the fluting of the side seam can be seen quite clearly.

In a bodice without a CB seam, the fit *down the CB* will be less smooth and close to the figure; but the effect of the waist darts, now increased to replace CB shaping, will still be the same as far as fluting of the side seam is concerned.

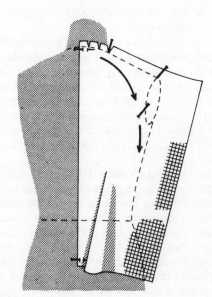

FIG. 16/1

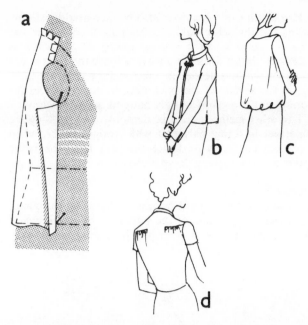

It is often useful, and even necessary, to have the surplus fullness moved from the top into the hem. It may be required **for some styles**, e.g. those with a 'swing-away back' (like swagger coats) or a pouched back (details *b*, *c*). It may also be useful **for some shapes of figure** when the silhouette, *seen sideways*, is not straight down the CB, but *slopes out* definitely towards the hips (erect or sway-back figure with a prominent seat). On such a figure a perfectly straight bodice back would tend to 'catch' on the hips and ride up into the waist. In such cases, however, it is not usual to transfer into the hem *the whole* shoulder dart: this would make the hem far *too loose*. It is sufficient to use only *part of the dart*; and even this would be done mainly for larger figures (see Chapter Two). In an average case of 'sway-back' figure a similar effect can be obtained by 'flaring from the armhole', as described in the next exercise (VI). Transferring of the shoulderblade dart into the hem is therefore used mainly in style designing.

B—Surplus fullness moved into the top of the bodice.
It has already been mentioned that the shoulder and waist darts are in a sense complementary: the shoulder dart could be smoothed down into the waist (as in the previous example A) and taken out in a **deeper** waist dart (which in practice, however, is not an advantage); and the waist dart could be moved (as in Exercise I) up into the armhole, and from there into the shoulder, adding to the depth of the shoulder dart. Since it is not practical to have a deep shoulderblade dart, any extra fullness obtained in this way would generally be moved, at least partly, into the neckline, as between the shoulder and the neckline a fairly considerable amount can be suppressed. Thus all the surplus fullness can be con-

centrated in the top part of the bodice, leaving a **dartless**, close fitting waist (Fig. 17).

In practice this does not happen very often as there are not many styles requiring this effect (which incidentally underlines 'round-shoulderness'). Moreover, what is possible with a waist-length bodice becomes impossible in a hip-length (or full length) back: one cannot smooth the waist dart fullness upwards when the bodice continues below the waist, as can be easily ascertained if one tried to model this.

Therefore, although the whole surplus fullness is sometimes concentrated in the top in style designing (detail *d*), in fitting it is more usual to use only a small part of the waist 'dart' to increase the width across the top (e.g. as in the Slanted CB which by tightening the

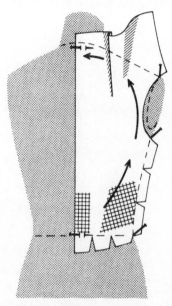

FIG. 17/I

waist increases the neckline width). Other methods of providing fullness across the top, not involving dart moving, will be described in the next exercise.

To sum up, therefore, **the most usual positions into which surplus back fullness can be moved** are the hemline (at waist or hip level), the shoulder, and the neckline, where it can often be *suppressed inconspicuously* (the main advantage). The surplus fullness is seldom, if ever, used in the side seam or CB (except sometimes in tailoring). The possibilities of manipulating this fullness are thus more limited in the back than in the front, where it can be moved to more positions and used for a greater variety of style and fitting effects.

EXERCISE VI—A STRAIGHT BACK WITH ADDITIONAL WIDTH
A—extra width in the hem
B—extra width in the top

Take a piece of leno 68 cm long and 35 cm wide and pin the selvedge to CB at the nape and hips, keeping it taut over the hollow of the waist. Model the top as usual, pinning out a shoulderblade dart. After marking UP, clearly outline the armhole and cut it out with turnings leaving, however, a bigger turning 2·5 cm in the lower part (Fig. 18).

On the hip level find HP, placing it in line with UP; fold the leno back in a straight (vertical) line and crease it between these two points. The crease, which is the side seam (not yet to be cut), may follow the SG or *slope out* slightly, according to the size of the hips. Note that at armhole level (i.e. the Bust line) the X–SG runs across in

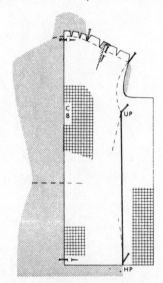

FIG. 18/1

a horizontal line: it is useful to mark it in coloured pencil. This completes **the modelling of a straight bodice back**.

The problem of **adding width (or fullness) to a straight back** will now be examined. Both *for style* and *for fit* this may be required either in the hem (whatever its level), or in the top part, i.e. across the shoulders and neckline. The swing-away hemline and the 'full shoulders' effect are two fashion lines which appear and disappear with changing fashion. It is also often necessary to add width to the hips or to the top **for different types of figure** (stooping, erect, etc.). Since the silhouette of the figure varies, the average *straight* line of the bodice will not fit everybody equally well.

A—Extra width in the hem.
There are several ways in which the hip width of a straight bodice can be increased and one of them was already demonstrated in the previous exercise—transferring shoulder dart into hem.

Hip width can, of course, also be increased by simply **letting out the sides seams**, i.e. sloping them out more. This is useful when *a general easing of hip width* is necessary; but it does not always achieve the right result when the width is needed in a particular part of the hips, e.g. in the *middle* of the back and, moreover, excessive sloping out can given an ugly hang to the side seams.

Two other methods must be demonstrated, as they are **important in fitting garments with straight backs**, when it is often necessary to detach the back from the figure and to allow it to hang down *without catching on the hips*.

Method I:
Returning to the straight bodice modelled on the stand, first mark the position of the side seam by pinning *next to it*, i.e. just outside it, a strip of leno selvedge (or very

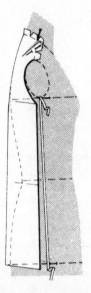

FIG. 19/1

narrow tape) between UP and HP, clearly indicating with a pin *placed horizontally* the *present level of UP*. Remove the two pins holding the side seam at UP and HP and *smooth the leno down the back armhole to 1 cm or over below* the present level (marked by the horizontal pin), allowing the side seam *to swing away* a little from its former line (marked by the tape). The seam will swing towards the back, thus detaching the back from the hips (Fig. 19): this will happen quite naturally as soon as UP is pushed down. The side seam can now be let out a little on the hips 1–2 cm to bring it back to its original vertical line and the armhole can be redrawn higher, i.e. to former UP level, using the wide turning.

Method 2:
Use the same leno model. After putting the side seam back to its former position (as it was before this last exercise), stab a pin into the armhole 9–10 cm above UP. Snip here a little into the turning of the armhole and from

this point drop a small 'flare' into the hem, pinning out on the hip line a fold 2–2·5 cm on the double (Fig. 20). The armhole line breaks and must be redrawn higher, using the turning. As the fold is pinned out, the side seam swings back and has to be let out to follow again the original vertical line marked by the tape. All this *loosens* the back in the middle part of the hips.

Although the new UP matches the front UP *on the stand* (the horizontal pin), it has actually been marked *higher* than the original one, as can easily be ascertained when the pattern is laid flat on the table (detail *a*). On the stand it will also be noted that the X–SG below the armhole now dips slightly towards the side, as it does also on the hemline, which has to be trimmed to match the front, i.e. to be parallel to the lower edge of the stand. The flat pattern (detail *a*) will actually curve up slightly at the hem.

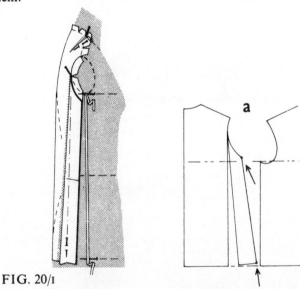

FIG. 20/I

In fact the *outline of the pattern changes* as does the grain. These changes are produced by the slight flaring from the armhole which releases tightness on the hips and gives the CB **a sloping-out line** when seen sideways, more suitable for some figures (sway-back, etc.). With the second method, used largely in tailoring for 'boxy' jackets and similar styles of coats, a little width is gained under the armhole which forms a draped fold much appreciated in this type of garment.

If, after these manipulations the total hip width is found to be excessive, some of the width added (usually about half) can again be taken out at the side seam, possibly equally on back and front, watching, however, to see that no drag develops from the shoulder blade (this is best tested on the figure). The main object of the operation was *to swing UP up* and so to produce a slight flare from the armhole, which detaches the *middle* of the back from the figure: letting out on the sides would not have had the same effect.

B—Extra width across the top of the back.

Pin the CB line as in the previous exercise; then, before proceeding to model the neckline, pin out a fold in the neck, 5–7·5 cm deep for example (this varies). Complete the top and finally the side seam by folding back the leno in a straight line from UP (Fig. 21). The X–SG, instead of running horizontally across, will now tend **to slope up** towards the armhole. The hem, which does likewise, may have to be adjusted. The fullness, according to the amount added, will run off to nothing higher or lower down the back.

The general effect of this silhouette, which is the reverse of the previous one, is a full top and by contrast a tight hem, with **a sloping-in CB line** (detail *b*). There are many styles requiring fullness in the top and at times

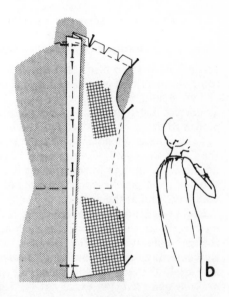

FIG. 21/I

this line is very fashionable. The extra fullness may be slight, just enough to give the back a sloping-in line; or it may be considerable, added in the neck and on the shoulders and, according to the style, taken out in gathers, folds, or darts.

In fitting a similar treatment of the bodice may be useful for a figure with prominent shoulder blades, round back or simply thick across the back shoulders: in such

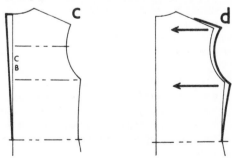

cases, however, only a small amount of extra width (2·5 cm or less) is generally added to the half neckline in a flat pattern (as shown in detail *c*). Such a small addition is intended to give just enough extra width or *ease across the shoulder blades*, without any obvious fullness. When the addition has to be made *at an actual fitting* of a garment, this can be done only *from the side* (detail *d*), i.e. from beyond the armhole and possibly top of the underarm, unless the CB has a seam with sufficient turning to let out.

EXERCISE VII—BODICE FRONT SHAPED BY DARTS
Distribution of surplus bust fullness

There is no need to prove that the front of a bodice has some surplus fullness produced by the curve of the bust and waist, and one can therefore begin by demonstrating its correct distribution in an average bodice (it can be pinned to the back modelled in Exercise II).

Take a piece of leno 55 × 32 cm, place the selvedge to the CF of the stand, leaving about 12 cm *above* the CF neckline, i.e. enough to reach to the highest point of the shoulder, and pin the leno at the base of the neck, on the bust level, and at the waist.

Begin by cutting the neckline (Fig. 22). Use short cuts, moving the scissors upwards after each cut and smoothing the leno slightly *away from the neck*; or, alternatively, snip carefully into the turning of *a roughly cut neckline* and apply the leno well to the stand so as to *keep the neckline quite flat*. Pin exactly at NP (there must be no gap between NP and neck).

On the bust level adjust the leno so that the X–SG runs in **a horizontal line across the bust**. Use a temporary pin near the side to keep the leno in this position. This is **the dividing line** between the fullness which belongs to the top part of the bodice, i.e. the shoulder dart, and the fullness of the lower part to be taken out in the waist.

Smooth the leno from the underarm up into the armhole, and from there—leaving the armhole quite flat—into the shoulder, where it is *pinned out as a dart*, the depth of which will vary not only according to the *size* of the bust, but also according to its *shape* (Fig. 23). Place the dart approximately in the middle of the shoulder, sloping it a little towards the CF and running it off just above the highest point of the bust—Fig. 24.

At the waist the surplus fullness is taken out in a dart placed *in line* with the shoulder dart. About 5 cm below the shoulder dart point the leno is creased along the L–SG down to the waist, and a 2·5–4 cm dart is taken out at the waist (Fig. 24).

Complete the side seam, folding the leno back in a straight line and allowing it *to fall naturally down the side*. It can, at this point, be pinned to the back (if a back is used). If this leaves some fullness in the waist (a small amount may be disregarded in a dress bodice), then one must decide if this fullness can be *smoothed naturally* into the side seam or not. If pushing this waist fullness into the underarm produces a diagonal crease from the bust point (detail *a*), then it must be smoothed *in the opposite direction* and added to the waist dart, increasing its depth. The amount of such extra waist fullness, over and above an *average* waist dart, depends on the hollow of the waist: this is often bigger than average e.g. on a figure with a higher bust. (See Chapter Two.)

The effect of this manipulation is, in fact, similar to eliminating the diagonal drag in the back of a bodice when dealing with a shoulder blade higher than usual, i.e. *letting out the side seam* and increasing the waist dart instead.

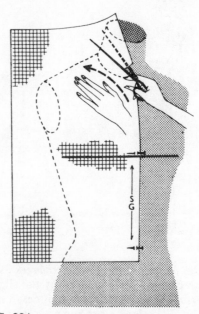

FIG. 22/I

Much depends on the actual shape of the figure: *the flatter it is, the more the side seam—back and front—can be taken in*, i.e. slanted, and vice versa, *the higher the bust and shoulder blade, the less one should attempt to pull in the waist*.

The waist dart fullness therefore often appears excessive, but it can be divided in various ways, both to avoid 'over-shaping' the figure by *too deep* a single dart and to make it easier to manage the darts, i.e. to run them off neatly. Some waist width can be suppressed by folding back 1·5 cm at the CF waist (the Sl.CF). A second dart is sometimes placed half-way between the basic one and the side seam (e.g. in tailoring). The waist dart can also be divided into several tucks, small darts or even eased into

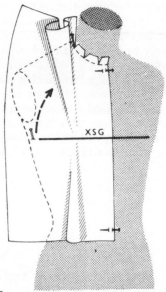

FIG. 23/I

the skirt waist of a dress, or enclosed in a Panel seam. Here, however, the **fitting problem of excessive depth** remains: so that generally only *part* of a deep waist dart is enclosed in a panel.

A useful observation to be made from this exercise is **that eliminating all surplus fullness from the armhole and neckline**, i.e. leaving them *quite flat*, results in a **deeper shoulder dart**. Therefore, conversely, any neckline or armhole looseness can generally be traced to the basic darts not being deep enough. However, here again the problem

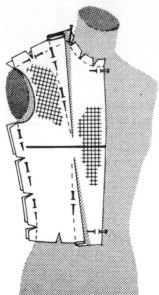

FIG. 24/I

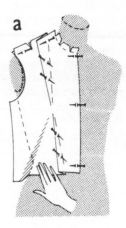

of distributing the surplus fullness to avoid overshaping and other technical difficulties, such as 'poking' darts, must always be borne in mind by the fitter: in some cases it may be advisable to leave the neckline, and even the armhole, a little loose in order to reduce a big dart.

If this bodice is continued to hip level or even 15 cm below the waist, the waist dart runs off on this level. The lower edge of the bodice follows the X–SG (except for CF dip).

EXERCISE VIII—BODICE FRONT WITH UNDERARM DART
Effect of bust fullness moved into the side seam

Begin by modelling a short front as described in the previous exercise (VII). Cut out neckline, pin at NP, set the X–SG in a horizontal line on bust level. Then, starting from NP, smooth the leno along the shoulder towards the armhole and, after pinning at SP, down the armhole into the side seam: a certain amount of fullness now appears below UP (Fig. 25). This is **the shoulder dart transferred into the underarm**. Here it can be suppressed either in its classical position, on the bust level, or in some other part of the side seam.

For **the basic position**, 4–5 cm below the armhole level, pin out the fullness in **a horizontal dart** from the side seam, going straight across to the highest point of the bust. Although it is easiest to pin the dart long enough to reach the bust point, this is actually seldom done in practice because such a long dart is considered unattractive, too conspicuous and likely to interfere with other lines of the style. It is generally *shortened* and made to run off to nothing 5–7 cm before reaching the bust point (detail *a*).

The *shortening of the underarm dart* may create a *minor fitting problem*, as a shortened dart always leaves some fullness (looseness) at its point, and since this fullness does not come to the highest part of the bust where it would have *distributed itself*, it tends to show as unnecessary 'puffiness' at *the side* of the bust. In some materials it can be shrunk away by pressing; in other cases, if objected to, it can be cleared only by pinning out i.e. by lengthening the dart again. The single underarm dart can of course be divided into two, but this does not always improve the situation.

It will be easily understood that this trouble is more likely to arise with a larger figure or one with a very high bust. In such cases, therefore, it is advisable to take

upwards, probably the most popular of them being the long diagonal or **slanted dart** (detail *c*), taken from a point at or a little above the waist and running in the direction of the bust. As the base of this dart is further away from the bust point, the dart can be made longer, and therefore deeper, without causing the difficulties connected with the basic position.

In this exercise it will be noted that **the grain** in the *lower part* of the bodice is in no way displaced and the waistline follows the X–SG, as in the previous exercise (VII). However, *at the top* there is a complete change as far as the grain is concerned. In the *absence of a shoulder dart*, the X–SG can run straight across from CF to arm-

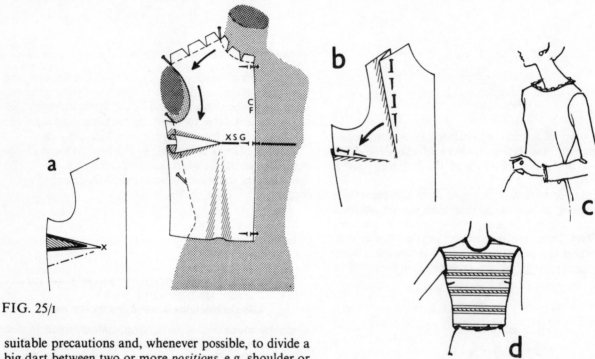

FIG. 25/I

suitable precautions and, whenever possible, to divide a big dart between two or more *positions*, e.g. shoulder or neckline with **additional underarm dart** (detail *b*).

Generally speaking this is a very good dart position for the smaller or flatter figure. For the larger figure, with a prominent bust, the shoulder dart is more suitable, for, even when it does not quite reach the bust point, it releases the fullness *just above*, where it is needed, and where it easily distributes itself.

On the other hand, as already stated, in the fitting of larger figures the underarm dart has a very important part to play as *an additional dart*. Most fitters take full advantage of it when it is necessary, for instance, to tighten an untidy front armhole by moving the fullness down into the side seam, rather than adding it to the main shoulder dart (see Chapter Two).

There are several other positions suitable for the underarm dart usually placed lower down the seam and sloping

hole (detail *d*). This may be quite an important consideration in planning a design, particularly in some fabrics, e.g. those with checks, plaids, stripes. A front with an underarm dart is therefore very popular with designers when such materials are in fashion.

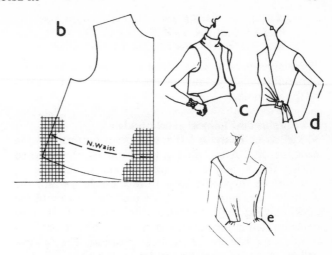

EXERCISE IX—FRONT WITHOUT DARTS OR ONLY A WAIST DART
Effect of surplus fullness moved into the hem

A—Bodice front without darts

Take a longer and wider piece of leno (about 40 cm wide) and pin, as usual down the CF. Cut out neckline and, after pinning at NP, smooth the leno along the shoulder and then down the armhole, exactly as in the previous exercise. Pin at UP, cutting and leaving the armhole quite flat (Fig. 26).

At the side let the leno fall in a straight line *over the waist hollow*. Fold it back for the seam in line with UP and pin 8–10 cm below the waist (Fig. 26).

The leno must fall quite naturally, as it wants to go. To test this, note that excessive pulling sideways (away

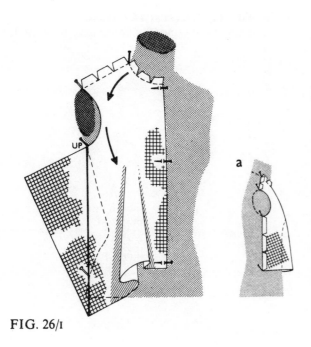

FIG. 26/1

from CF) will produce diagonal creases from the direction of the bust, which of course must be avoided. After pinning the side seam to the stand correctly, i.e. without forcing it towards the side, it will be noted that *below the bust* there appears a certain amount of fullness which is in excess of the usual waist dart fullness. This is how the **shoulder dart fullness** appears when **transferred into the hem** (detail *a*).

It will be observed that the *lower edge of the leno rectangle*, which is on X–SG, now *dips* towards the side, so that *a new hemline* has to be drawn, measuring it up from the lower edge of the stand. This hem, as well as the waistline, will be completely 'off the grain'. In this it differs from the bodices modelled so far (Exercise VII

and VIII). When the pattern is examined flat on the table (detail *b*), it will be seen that the *side seam slopes out* considerably and that both hem and waistline are *curved*.

The extra width which develops below the waist gives the front a 'swing-out' effect which increases with length, though it hardly shows in a short bodice with the hem level above the waist (e.g. a bolero). Therefore, in a very short bodice it can be ignored (detail *c*). In a longer (or waist-length) bodice the fullness either *hangs away*, or is gathered into a pouch or sometimes draped (detail *d*): there are different ways of dealing with it (see also section B below).

In fitting this effect may be useful for a certain shape of figure—a figure with a prominent abdomen. In such a case, however, it is not usual to transfer the *whole* of the shoulder dart, but only part of it (e.g. $\frac{1}{4}$ or $\frac{1}{3}$) sufficient to make the front stand away just a little from the figure.

B—Bodice front with a waist dart only.

This is modelled in exactly the same way, but as this is always a waist-length and close fitting bodice, the side seam is applied to the figure and pinned *at the waist*, without allowing any 'pull' to develop from the bust level.

The transferred bust dart fullness combines with the original waist dart and can be taken out in **one deep dart at the waist**: this large dart can of course be split into two or even three smaller darts, if desired (detail *e*). This version is particularly suitable for close fitting bodice styles, such as are often used in theatrical designing (ballet costumes, period dresses, etc.). As in version A, the side is quite 'off the grain' and so is the lower edge of the curved waistline.

N.B. This pattern, with the bust dart fullness in the waist, was **in the past the generally accepted foundation** pattern (bodice block) and drafting methods were consequently adapted to its outline, proportions and grain position. It is still used by some cutters and designers.

EXERCISE X—FRONT WITH SURPLUS FULLNESS IN VARIOUS POSITIONS
Bust dart fullness in the neckline or CF or armhole

There are several other positions to which the Shoulder dart fullness can be moved: the neckline, the CF seam or the armhole.

A—Surplus bust fullness in the neckline.

Model as in Exercise VII but without cutting out the neckline first. After pinning to CF, as usual, and then setting the X–SG to a horizontal line on bust level, smooth the surplus fullness from the side up into the armhole, then into the shoulder and from there into the neckline (Fig. 27). Note that the amount of fullness concentrated in the neckline is considerable, in fact only a little less than in the shoulder position. The fullness will be arranged and the neckline cut out according to the style (details *a*, *b*).

It is sometimes necessary to have only *part of the bust dart fullness* in the neckline, just enough to 'ease' it, but without producing any visible gathers. The rest of the dart is then used in some other position, e.g. in the underarm. Such **neckline loosening** may be essential for some styles, e.g. those with a *built-up neckline* or draped fold at the base of the neck: without this precaution it may work out too tight. On some figures, e.g. with *forward sloping neck*, this can be quite a serious defect.

Retaining a little of the surplus fullness in the neckline is often very useful because it can so easily be disposed of there, for instance even under a collar. Not only is this quite becoming, but it also **helps to reduce the depth of the basic dart**, sometimes an important consideration for a fitter. However, one must know when this is likely to be helpful and when, on the contrary, this may spoil the fit of a neckline (see Chapter Four).

B—Surplus bust fullness in a CF seam.

This position is obtained by continuing to smooth the

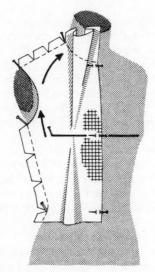

FIG. 27/I

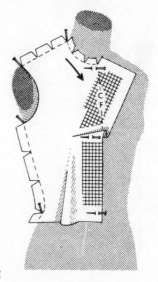

FIG. 28/I

There are not many fitting problems in these styles for they are generally becoming and often very suitable for figures with a high bust, because the fullness comes over the CF where there may be tightness which this fullness helps to ease.

fullness of the neckline down into the CF as far as the bust level (Fig. 28). Up to this point the modelling is identical with the previous exercise.

It will be noted that the amount of fullness which appears on the CF is smaller than the amount obtained in the neckline, even though it is *the same bust dart*. The reason is quite simple: the depth of a dart and hence the fullness it provides, depends on its length, i.e. on its distance from the highest point of the bust (X). The same dart will therefore appear bigger or smaller according to *how far it has to run* from bust point to one of the outer edges—side seam, shoulder, etc.

This is an interesting detail to note, as some use is made of it both in designing and fitting. In designing it may provide a method for 'concealing' the bust dart which can be made to disappear completely in a band edging the fronts or under a narrow CF panel or tab. In fitting, it may be an easy way of eliminating the bust dart on a small, flat-chested figure.

C—Surplus bust fullness in the armhole.

This is on the whole a less frequently used position for the bust dart, though at times it becomes popular, particularly when enclosed in a curved panel seam from the armhole.

The modelling of such a bodice would be similar to Exercise VIII, with the fullness taken out in a dart starting from somewhere near the chest level and pointing towards the bust (Fig. 29).

In fitting, almost the only problem is that it is frequently necessary *to increase the depth of this dart*, particularly when it is enclosed in a panel seam (detail *c*). The most likely explanation is that the dart starts in *a hollow*. Any

EXERCISE XI—STYLES WITH BUST AND WAIST DARTS COMBINED
Concentrating all surplus fullness in one position

Model a front dividing the surplus dart fullness as usual between shoulder and waist. Outline the armhole in coloured pencil but *without cutting* it.

Instead of taking out the lower fullness in the usual waist dart, move it sideways towards the seam. It has already been shown in a previous exercise (VII) that this fullness cannot be pushed into the side seam without producing a drag or crease from the bust point. It will be found, however, that if it is *taken out in a slanted dart pointing towards the bust* (as the crease actually runs), the result is quite satisfactory. This in fact represents the waist fullness moved to **a diagonal underarm position**, which on the whole is very popular (Fig. 30).

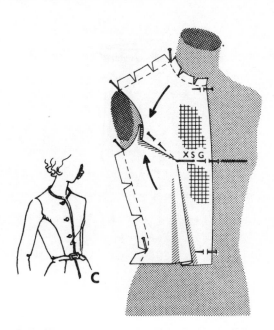

FIG. 29/ɪ

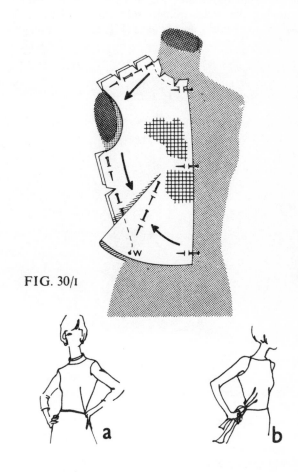

FIG. 30/ɪ

seam or dart crossing this hollow may need tightening to follow the actual shape of the figure, whereas without any seam (or dart) the armhole just *drapes* over it.

After undoing the shoulder dart, move the bust fullness towards the armhole and down into the side seam to *join the diagonal dart* which, of course, will be increased in depth. **The two darts are now combined in the same position** (details *a* and *b*).

In the same way the waist dart fullness can be moved in the opposite direction, towards the CF and then up *a CF seam* to join the bust fullness brought down from the neckline (Fig. 31). This increases the amount of fullness on the CF and provides a *more definite draped effect* (detail *d*), while at the same time leaving *the waist quite flat* (dartless).

c

Another example of **dart combination** is the **deeper cowl**: its depth and fullness can be increased substantially by moving the waist fullness into the neckline *to be added to the Shoulder dart fullness* (Fig. 32). This must be

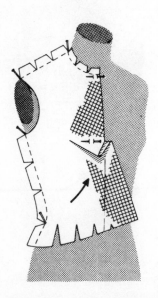

FIG. 31/I

done through the side seam and the armhole to retain a correct CF line, i.e. 'to the fold' (either SG or more usually true bias). It will be noted that this gives a deeper and fuller (more draped) cowl than if only the Shoulder dart alone were used in this way (detail *c*).

Altogether there are **a number of possible combinations** providing much scope for designing and often quite useful in fitting. Style effects which are difficult or even impossible to achieve with the use of the bust dart alone, become quite easy when the waist dart is combined with it.

It must be noted that with the moving of the surplus fullness **the grain position may be altered** and X–SG may no longer run in a horizontal line across the bust. The

grain is already upset when the bust dart is moved into the underarm *below the bust level*, e.g. to a diagonal dart, and of course when it is moved into the waist (Exercise IX) to join the waist dart: this is already a case of 'combined dart'.

With regard to problems of fit, some of these manipulations may be of help when dealing with a certain

d

shape of figure. A figure with a prominent bust is often more hollow *under the bust*, so that the front tends *to hang away* (as if requiring a deeper waist dart). Some of this excess width can with advantage be moved sideways to

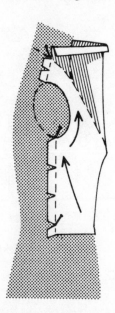

FIG. 32/I

the underarm (creases from bust appear), and then *up the side seam* (until creases disappear again), to be *added to an existing underarm dart*, or to introduce a new dart *in addition* to the shoulder dart (see Chapter II—Fig. 26). **N.B.** It is interesting to mention at this stage that **combining back dart fullness** is also possible. In fact, examples of this have already been given in Exercises I and V.

EXERCISE XII—BODICE WITH INCREASED DART FULLNESS
Increasing the darts for a closer fit to the figure

Model a simple front with the usual bust and waist darts and join it to a back (the back and front modelled in Exercises II and VII can be used). If the top of this bodice is cut away 8 cm above bust level (or simply unpinned at the shoulder and folded down), it will be found (Fig. 33) that the top edge is quite loose (allow for the stiffness of the leno). This will be even more so on a figure because it is not rigid like the stand. The usual bust dart does not make *the top edge* (i.e. the chest level) sufficiently tight *to keep the bodice up without the support of the shoulder section*. This makes it unsuitable for some styles, e.g. for a strapless evening bodice (detail *a*). It will have to be **tightened**, i.e. taken in, not just on the side seams, but also and mainly **above the curve of the bust**, thus **increasing the basic dart**.

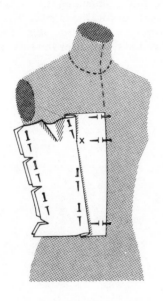

FIG. 33/I

Another suitable example of this would be an evening dress bodice designed on 'brassiere' lines, e.g. for a high-waisted Empire line dress (detail *b*). With the usual bust dart it would not fit close enough to the actual curve of the figure, as required by the style.

Pin a piece of leno (21–25 cm wide) flat to the side seam of the stand, as shown in Fig. 34, then mould it *round the bust* smoothing all surplus fullness towards the CF and leaving *no loose edge above* and below. Cut away surplus beyond CF. Much more fullness will be obtained on the CF than in a previous examples (Exercise X–B). If instead of being 'draped', the fullness is taken out in a single CF dat, it will be found that it is—though short—quite a deep one. **With the closer fit to the bust the surplus fullness has increased**.

Yet another example one comes across in fitting is the case of **the very cut out neckline** which tends to slip off the shoulders. Here a *preliminary tightening of the top of the bodice*, by increasing the bust dart, helps to keep the neckline flatter and *more clinging to the figure* (see also Chapter IV). In modelling the top part, the fabric is smoothed *away from the neck* and applied very flat, almost tight, *across the chest*, moving all surplus fullness into the underarm for example: a wide or deep neckline cut

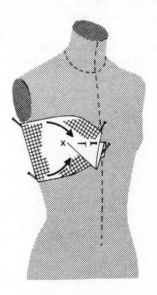

FIG. 34/I

out subsequently will have less tendency to stretch and fall off the shoulders than if some ease had been left *above* the bust. This naturally results in an increased dart in the underarm or wherever the dart is used.

It will be obvious from the above example that an increase of surplus fullness is unavoidable whenever *a more moulded fit to the bust part is required*, and also that an increased bust dart can be used *in any position*.

In all the above examples the problem of closer fit arises mainly because of the requirements of the style or type of garment; but it may also arise because of the shape of the figure. It is therefore useful to **distinguish two different cases**: *a*) when it is necessary **to increase the bust dart occasionally** for a special style or a fitting effect; and *b*) when it is necessary **to increase the bust dart permanently** to fit a bust which is higher than average.

Defects connected with this latter problem are discussed in Chapter Two (Shape of figure defects).

If, as an experiment, a pad is pinned to the stand over the bust to raise its height, as was done for the shoulder blade in Exercise I, the *armhole will become loose*, and by smoothing this unwanted fullness up into the shoulder dart, the latter will naturally be increased. A drag appearing from the bust down to side seam may also be eliminated by letting out the side seam and making the waist dart deeper instead—which is **another form of dart increase**. **N.B.** In this case bust and waist darts must be considered as contributing together towards *a more shaped silhouette* of the front.

It must be noted, however, that a deeper bust dart, though suitable, and even necessary, in some cases and for certain types of figure, is not *generally* becoming and suitable for everybody. Although a more clinging fit above the bust is useful for a big neckline or a strapless top, it tends to produce a strained, 'narrow-chested' effect and overshapes the bust. A *basic dart* should not be too deep, so that **a certain amount of ease or 'drape' over the hollow of the armhole** and across the chest **is retained**.

Moreover, a permanently deep dart may cause trouble in other ways, making, for example, the distribution and concealment of darts more difficult, or tightening the front armhole too much (see Chapter Three—armhole defects).

It is sometimes necessary **to reduce the basic dart** in order to achieve a looser, more draped fit in such garments as blouses, sports wear and various other casual clothes. Modelling patterns on the stand *does not mean moulding them always tightly* to the figure, and often there is the opposite problem of keeping the fit sufficiently loose. A little extra ease is often provided by 'pinning out' provisionally, when modelling, small amounts of fullness where necessary, e.g. on the chest.

When a style requires extra fullness beyond the small amount of ease referred to above, and the fullness must be added in such a way that it *does not increase the moulding and closer fit of the bust*, then this is done in the same way as explained for the back in Exercise VI, i.e. by **flaring** from one of the outer edges (armhole, neckline, shoulder) or simply **by introducing extra width** for pleats, tucks, gathers, folds, smocking, etc.—*right through* in the form of a 'pleat' or fold made in the leno. When fitting a garment, however, any *extra width* at this stage can come only from the turnings of the side seam, armhole or CF seam.

THE FITTING OF A BODICE

GENERAL REMARKS ON FITTING

Systematic fitting usually follows a definite plan and is based on an understanding of what causes various defects and on knowledge of how to remove them without spoiling the fit of the other parts of the garment.

Fittings are often troublesome because fitters do not consider sufficiently **the importance of the preliminary work** and the early stages of cutting out and assembling a garment which can do so much to complicate or to simplify a fitting. Where careless preparation is allowed or, for the sake of speed, encouraged, various defects may be due as much to faulty patterns, wrong cutting of material and careless assembling, as to a difficult or unusual shape of figure. The possibility of *several causes for every defect* obviously makes a fitting complicated and unreliable.

It is only by eliminating these extra possibilities that the work can be put on a reliable basis—a fact greatly appreciated in high class workrooms where fitters of experience are most particular about methodical preparation of garments for fittings.

Once the possibility of mistakes due to careless cutting out and assembling is eliminated, or at least reduced to a minimum, the fitting is mainly concerned with **defects** which are obviously **caused by irregularities in the shape of the figure**.

It should be mentioned here, however, that **when fitting actual garments**, and not just block patterns, there still remains another possible source of trouble: **defects due to wrong judgement in designing the pattern**, and various 'accidents' which cannot be entirely avoided, even by the most competent dressmakers. The lines and details of a style may not always have been successfully planned *for an individual figure*; stretching of material or loss of size through shrinkage, or puckering of seams may happen in the best of workrooms. The correction of these mistakes, however, rarely presents serious problems. In any case there is little one can learn about them *theoretically*, for they are connected not so much with principles of Cutting and Fitting, as with *skill* in handling the work and with the general *standard of workmanship*. Common sense, good taste and practical experience must be relied upon in dealing with such mistakes.

For theoretical study there remains, therefore, only the group of **defects caused by variations in the shape of the figure**.

FITTING A BODICE

The aim of a fitting should be:
(a) **to check the size** of the garment
(b) **to adjust the fit to the shape** of the figure
(c) **to check the lines of the style** so as to ensure the most becoming effect on the figure.

In fitting a bodice block only the first two points have to be considered. The third does not arise until the fitting of an actual garment, i.e. a style. The two first points, however, represent by far the most important part of a fitting.

The Fitting scheme given below deals with the fitting of a bodice, and more particularly a bodice block or a foundation pattern. It can, however, be taken as a **general basis for the fitting of any garment**.

It is obvious that where the garment is cut from a previously corrected foundation or *individual block*, the necessity for dealing with most of the points to be mentioned lower, will disappear. The same, of course, applies to sleeves and skirts. On the other hand, every fitting of a *garment*, as distinct from a foundation would, in addition, deal with the checking of the various lines of the style on the figure, and also with the 'behaviour' of the fabric, for a style may be suitable for one fabric but not for another. All this is part of a practical fitting of a garment but, as already explained, no hard and fast rules or, in fact, any theoretical instruction can be given for it, if only because of the endless variety of new materials and *constantly changing fashion*.

The bodice block must be cut out in a suitable fabric, such as a *soft* calico, a heavy type of mull, or a piece of old sheet (most suitable for this purpose). The fabric should be as much as possible like an ordinary *supple* dress material, with sufficient 'body' and weight, but without any heavy dressing which might produce extra creases, which are most confusing in this type of basic fitting.

After cutting out the bodice block with good turnings, the pattern is *carefully outlined* with lines crossing at all

THE FITTING SCHEME
FOR A BODICE

STAGE I   CHECKING MEASUREMENTS AND
                                        PROPORTIONS

On putting on the bodice survey the general effect and
carefully note the following:

1. Bust width, i.e. the fit round the bust
2. Back neckline—its width and depth
3. Front neckline—its width and depth
4. Chest width (about 12 cm below neckline)
5. Back width (between the armholes)
6. Shoulder length

Nothing should be corrected at this stage, only noted and,
if necessary, a measurement taken again. The whole
checking takes but a minute or two.

STAGE II   ADJUSTING THE BODICE TO THE
                                    SHAPE OF THE FIGURE

Now observe and check:

The distribution   7. The *relative* width of Front and Back at Bust level
of the Bust width

The fit of the   8. The shoulder—its slant and tightness
Back   9. The Balance, i.e. depth above the armhole
                           10. The fit to the shape or curves of the figure

The fit of the   11. The shoulder—its slant and tightness
Front   12. The Balance i.e. depth above the armhole
                           13. The fit to the curves of the figure

The shoulder seam can now be opened for any corrections.

After correcting the main defects

14. Check the armhole for shape and size
15. Check the waistline for fit and position
16. Check and outline the *final* neckline

important points such as NP, SP, UP, etc. It is then assembled, after matching these points which serve as 'balance marks': NP and SP for the shoulder seam, UP and HP for side seams, waistlines meeting. The shoulder darts and waist darts are tacked, and side seams are joined either on the *inner* or preferably on the *outer* lines, in order to test the *looser fit* first. Turnings are usually left inside, though in diagrams, for a clearer effect, they may sometimes be shown outside.

The *inner* shaped side seams and the Sl.CF and Sl.CB must be clearly marked, so that they can be *pinned out at the fitting to test the tighter fit* of the bodice.

The CF is usually left open, with 2·5–4 cm wrap or turning folded under the CF lines on the right side, and pinned over the left CF line when the bodice is on the figure.

It is important not to try to correct anything at an early stage, before the whole fit has been carefully surveyed: an early adjustment of a single defect may often upset something else or, on further consideration, even prove to be unnecessary: One should learn to get a quick picture of the whole situation, always bearing in mind that *one adjustment can often put right several defects.*

It must of course be understood that not every fitter will necessarily follow such a plan, or even a similar one. Methods of practical fitting vary considerably. The point to emphasize is that it is useful to have some plan in fitting and to try to keep to it, for concentrating just on the very obvious and overlooking a less noticeable, but basically important point is precisely that which so often shows up an inexperienced fitter. In this respect the fitting of a block is particularly good practice because it is so obvious that overlooking a defect in a block means making the block pattern less reliable for future use.

The explanations of the various points mentioned in the Fitting Scheme which now follow are intended to provide the basic knowledge which helps a fitter to form—almost at a glance—a general picture of the whole situation. Without it a Fitting Scheme can be of little value.

EXPLANATIONS OF THE VARIOUS POINTS OF THE FITTING SCHEME

STAGE I

CHECKING MEASUREMENTS AND PROPORTIONS

THE BUST WIDTH—*point 1*—seldom needs altering in a bodice block drafted to correct measurements; but it may appear a little too loose on a small or too tight on a large figure if the precaution had not been taken to measure according to size, i.e. tighter for a smaller and looser for a larger person (this requires some experience). If, however, the width does look wrong, take the measurement again and adjust pattern accordingly, preferably later on the flat.

When it is necessary to make an adjustment of the bust width *on the figure* (this will of course happen more often with garments than with block patterns), then, since generally only one side of the bodice is fitted (let out or taken in), allowance *must be made* for the increase or decrease on the other side before the final result can be *visualized*. The idea of fitting one side only is to enable *corrections to be transferred to the other side more accurately.* Only if the figure is seen to be very uneven would an adjustment be made on both sides during a fitting, but this seldom happens with the bust width.

A bodice block must not fit tightly but have the **easy fit of an ordinary dress bodice.** If it is prepared for the fitting along its *outer* side seams, it may of course appear somewhat loose. It should then be pinned on its inner side seams and have the Sl.CF and CB pinned out (the latter are treated here as 'darts' but will later be used as required by style). All this tightens the bodice considerably, not only at the waist but also *round the bust.* Only after this can one judge whether the width is still excessive, in which case it can be adjusted at the side seam. Incidentally, at this stage it may also be found that the Sl.CF, when pinned out, is unsuitable, i.e. too tight across the front waist, for some figures.

N.B. When fitting dresses it may happen that the bust width is wrong even after using a perfectly correct foundation. This may be due to the fabric (too bulky, too clinging, too easily stretched); or to careless assembling, when garments are allowed to 'grow' or lose size; or to some peculiar detail of cut and style; but, most frequently to a misjudgement of extra width allowance when designing the pattern.

THE BACK NECKLINE—*point 2*—is important because it **controls the position of the shoulder seam.** The *basic* neckline should fit *well up to the neck* at CB and NP, even if later it is to be cut away from the neck to follow style or fashion. A little ease in the neckline can always be allowed and is even *essential for some figures,* provided it is held in, i.e. *pinned out at the fitting,* to be eased into the neckline later.

Some figures with an overdeveloped nape or with very round back and shoulders require more width or ease in the back neckline to release the strain *across* the nape. Such extra width, sometimes transferred from the shoulderblade dart, sometimes additional to it, is *smoothed from the shoulder towards the neck* and pinned

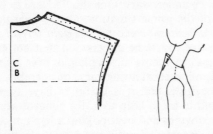

FIG. 1/II

out in the neckline (Fig. 1) when the shoulder seam is opened for corrections (after point 13). The shoulder seam is then re-adjusted.

THE FRONT NECKLINE—*point 3*—is controlled by the back neckline as far as the sides (NP's) are concerned; but it must have the **right depth for the shape or slope of the neck** which may be average, i.e. *straight*, or *forward sloping* (Fig. 2). Mark the correct CF depth (pit of neck) with a pin, the whole neckline to be finally outlined at the end of the fitting.

Any *looseness* observed in the front neckline must be considered as *part of the Shoulder dart* into which it can always be moved to obtain a flat neckline fit (see Modelling Exercise VII). It may be left intentionally in the neckline because, for some figures, this is quite suitable and also helps to reduce the size of the Shoulder dart (see also explanations of point 7 below). On the other hand this may spoil the shape of some necklines, as explained in Chapter Four. At this early stage it is usually just noted. If excessive, it may be corrected when the shoulder is opened (after point 13).

THE BACK WIDTH, CHEST WIDTH AND SHOULDER LENGTH—*points 4, 5, 6*—must be quickly checked and, if necessary, remeasured, remembering that a sleeve cannot be set in and fitted correctly if these measurements are wrong. It must also be borne in mind that when a person is first measured, there is a tendency to assume an unnatural posture, often more upright than usual. At a fitting, standing more naturally, it is sometimes found that the measurements are slightly out. However, the final checking and outlining of the armhole (point 14) should finally fix them all quite correctly.

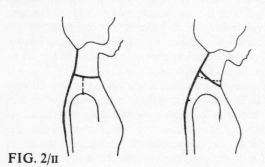

FIG. 2/II

STAGE II

ADJUSTING THE BODICE TO THE SHAPE OF THE FIGURE

Here again the various defects should at first be only noted. Except for Bust width distribution (point 7), and sometimes the actual Bust width (point 1) which, if more convenient, can be adjusted at an early stage, correcting begins only after checking point 13, when the shoulder seam is opened.

DISTRIBUTION OF BUST WIDTH—*point 7*. While the **total bust width** depends on the **measurement** of the figure, **the way it is distributed between back and front** depends mainly on **the shape** of the figure.

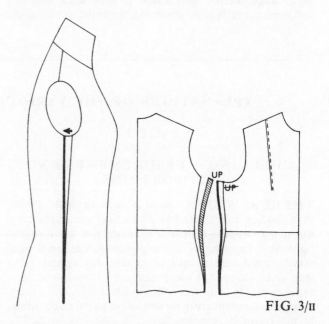

FIG. 3/II

In connection with this one must consider 3 possible defects:
A—wrong position of the underarm (or side) seam;
B—Looseness of back while the front is correct;
C—Tightness of front while the back is correct.
A—**The underarm seam** UP–HP on the figure should be in the middle of the underarm or very slightly to the back. It should run in a vertical or almost vertical line. If it appears to **slope forward at the top**, then UP can be moved back a little (0·5–1 cm) to straighten the line (Fig. 3). The HP is seldom touched, unless its actual position *on the figure* appears to be quite wrong.

The moving back of UP is not a frequent correction, but does occur on some figures, e.g. on small figures with extra wide chest and back and a *narrow underarm part*, also on some large figures with a prominent bust and

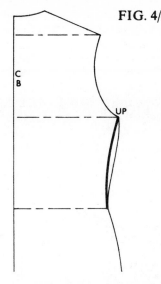

FIG. 4/II

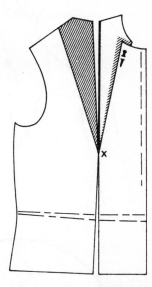

FIG. 6/II

wide chest; or, in general, when in drafting the block, too much width had been allocated to the Back between CB and UP.

N.B. It must be remembered, however, that here a *bodice block with a standard side seam* is being fitted. In various styles—both in dressmaking and tailoring—the underarm seam may be moved from its central or almost central position to suit the *requirements of the design*.

B—When the back appears loose (at bust level) while the front is correct, one must always see first that all the waist darts, the S1.CB and the *inner* side seam are pinned out *before judging the final effect*. Check also to see if the **back side seam** has been sufficiently curved inwards between UP and the waist, as an unnecessary 'bulge' here (so popular in many trade patterns) may often be the cause of untidy looseness under the arm (Fig. 4). In a properly balanced pattern with *sufficient basic width* well distributed round the bust, this 'bulge' at the side seam can be justified only if the figure is actually fat under the arms. The average or small figure does not need it and, on the contrary, often requires a more hollowed out line for a closer fit to the side curve of the back.

When all this does not correct the defect, it is advisable to move the whole side seam back slightly: this will reduce the width of the back (while increasing that of the front) and so place the seam in a better position for a *closer fit to the side hollow* of the back.

C—When the front appears tight across the bust and chest so that there is even difficulty in making the front edges meet, while on the other hand there is evidence that the **total** bust width is sufficient (the back may even be slightly loose), it is a case of **wrong width distribution**. In this case **widen the middle of the front** to bring more ease over the prominent bust or abdomen, reducing instead the width under the arms.

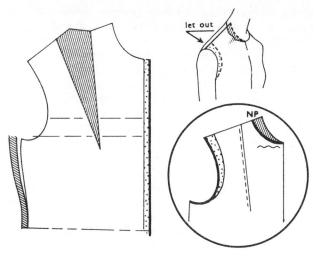

FIG. 5/II

The pattern correction in Fig. 5 shows this very clearly: a strip 0·5–1 cm wide is added down the CF and at the side seam the same width is cut away. Where the back appears to be correct, take it entirely off the front side seam (as in Fig. 5); but if the back is slightly loose reduce equally on both edges of the side seam, or sometimes even on the back only. The thing to remember is that *the total bust width must not be changed*: only more of it must be made to come over the CF.

The resulting *extra neckline width* can be dealt with by manipulation, e.g. easing under a collar or into a *suitable* fancy neckline. It can also be moved out of the neckline into the Shoulder dart or sometimes even into the hem (Fig. 6), which is often quite suitable for a figure with a big abdomen and wide hips (see Shape of figure defects later).

At an actual fitting move the whole front shoulder towards the neck and cut out neckline more at NP, dealing with the wider neckline as explained above (but mainly by easing); then *lengthen shoulder* and *widen the chest* at the armhole: this throws more width into the chest part and reduces the underarm width exactly as the adding of the strip to the CF of the pattern does (see detail in Fig. 5).

Defects connected with further points—8, 9, 10, 11, 12 and 13—will be examined in 3 groups.

GROUP I   —**Shoulder defects**
GROUP II   —**Balance defects**
GROUP III —**Shape of figure defects**

In many cases these defects appear in various combinations but it is best at first to study each group separately.

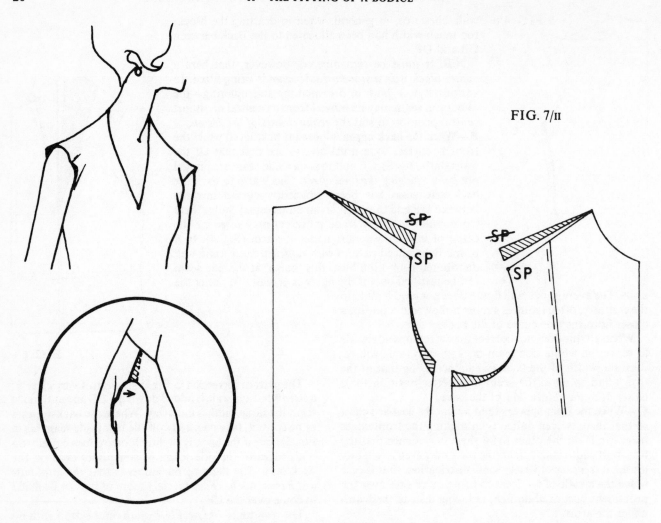

FIG. 7/II

GROUP I—SHOULDER DEFECTS

SLOPING SHOULDERS

When the figure has sloping shoulders, the fit of the shoulder seam is loose near the armhole and generally tight at the neck. Two different cases, however, must be considered:

A—**The simplest case** is when the fit near the neck is reasonably satisfactory, but **near the armhole the shoulder is definitely loose**, sometimes only slightly, but usually enough to cause the armhole to 'sag' and crease, as if with excess length. The shoulder end seems to need tightening to pull up the armhole and clear the creases (sketch and Fig. 7). This is what is actually done: the shoulder is taken up at SP, running the line off at NP.

N.B. Corrections in the diagrams are mostly shown both **for the bodice**, where everything depends on turnings (seam allowance), and **for the pattern**, where one can actually cut away or add paper, as required by the alteration.

The amount taken in at SP may sometimes be quite small, just 0·5–1 cm (to pull up armhole), but often considerably more. It may be taken *equally from back and front*, or more from one side than the other, or even entirely from one edge of the seam: this would depend on the actual position or 'run' of the shoulder seam *on the figure*. Therefore, as well as **tightening the shoulder at SP** there may be also an **adjustment of the shoulder line** to suit the shape of the figure (detail).

Since taking up at SP *reduces the armhole*, the latter must be adjusted to its former size (assuming that this size *was correct*) by lowering it down the underarm. This applies, however, only to a noticeably sloping shoulder and to considerable tightening at SP: a small amount can be disregarded until the armhole—its shape and size—are finally checked at the end of the fitting.

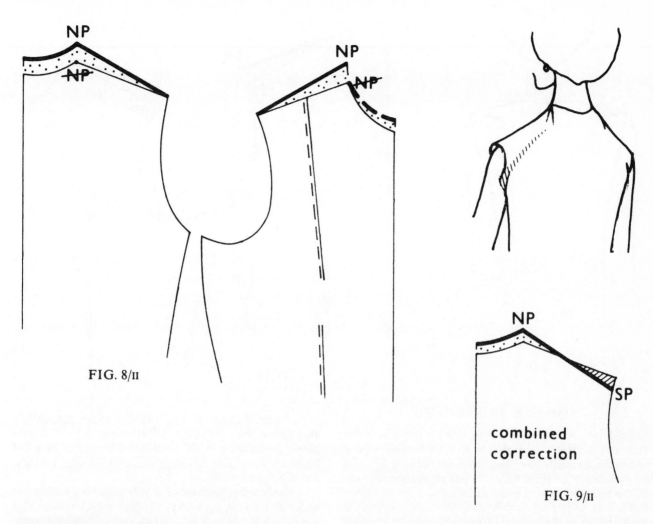

FIG. 8/II

combined
correction

FIG. 9/II

B—The other case of sloping shoulders is connected with what is generally described as a 'long neck' (or bottle neck) figure, usually with well developed muscles at the base of the neck. The **fit of the shoulders appears definitely tight at NP** and this tightness makes the armhole end loose. This suggests the **correction**: letting out at NP (0·5–1 cm, sometimes more) until the armhole end settles down and the looseness there almost or completely disappears (Fig. 8). In this case no lowering of the armhole on the underarm is necessary, and any further tightening can always be done *additionally at SP*. In an emergency, when fitting a bodice with insufficient turnings, the two methods are usually combined (Fig. 9). This should in any case be done whenever the letting out required at NP appears *excessive* and there is reason to fear that it *may affect the 'balance' of the bodice* (see Balance defects).

Letting out at NP is done either *equally* on back and front (no change in balance), or more is let out at the back NP, or at the front NP (in both cases with a change

in balance), according to the requirements of the shape and posture of the figure. It is a frequent correction at fittings, partly because other defects (i.e. mainly balance defects) can be corrected at the same time.

Fashion note on sloping shoulders.
It must be noted that **fashion affects the fitting of shoulders** to a considerable degree. At certain periods particular adjustments of the shoulder line become more frequent and important than others. When natural, i.e. more sloping shoulders are in fashion, it is found that it is more usual at a fitting to have to tighten the shoulder at SP and/or to loosen it at NP, which means that the **slope of the shoulder is more often increased**. At such times the frequent 'tightness' observed at NP is probably largely due to a more 'relaxed' posture and to a tendency to stoop and to allow the shoulders to droop, which, in fact, is a natural response to the influence of the current fashion silhouette.

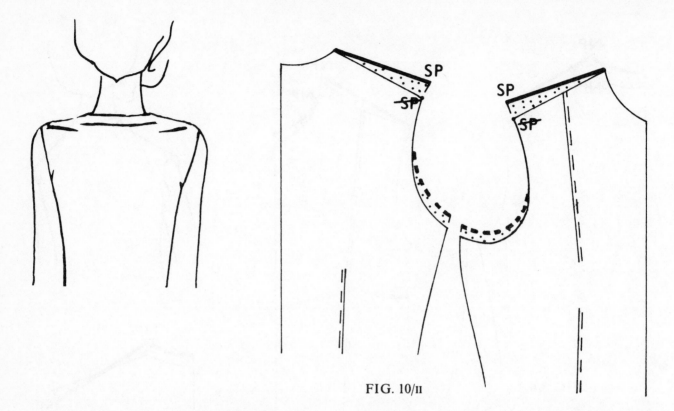

FIG. 10/II

SQUARE SHOULDERS

Shoulders which are higher than average at the armhole end are described as 'square'. With such shoulders there is usually tightness over the shoulder bone at SP, and as a consequence there may be **a pull right across the top of the back**, between the left and right SP, which causes fullness to be *pushed up* in horizontal folds towards the neck and under the collar. In front there may be a pulling away of front edges or of a cut-out (e.g. V-shaped) neck-line. Generally speaking the shoulder section feels **tight over the shoulder bone and loose at the neck**, and may even stand away from it, so that it seems that this looseness could easily be cleared by taking the bodice up at NP.

The more correct and safe way is to **let it out at SP** (Fig. 10) until the shoulder part near the neck settles down and the looseness at NP disappears (or almost), together with any drags across the top of the back and chest. This is generally sufficient in all but the more serious cases, and it is seldom necessary, or advisable, to take up at NP except for *figures with short, straight backs*, or, of course, in emergency cases where the turnings at the armhole end are insufficient.

When, however, the defect appears on a figure with a short, flat back and upright carriage, it is quite correct to *reduce the depth of the back* a little by taking it up at NP (Fig. 11). This not only changes the slope of the shoulder line, i.e. squares it, but also *affects the balance of the*

bodice (see Balance defects). It is a more responsible adjustment than the simple letting out at SP which only causes an increase in the armhole: this may or may not be desirable, but at this stage can generally be put right again by raising UP.

A combined adjustment (Fig. 12) involving letting out at SP and taking up at NP—in each case less than if it were done at one end only—is also often a suitable solution of this problem, particularly *where turnings are insufficient*.

From the above example it is already clear how important it is not to concentrate on the shoulder defect alone, without, at the same time, observing the shape and posture of the figure as a whole. Careful preliminary checking and observation always prove their value at this stage.

It is also clear that **good turnings** in the shoulder seam are of considerable importance, particularly when fitting an actual garment; though, on the other hand, cutting from *a corrected personal block* will reduce considerably any danger of insufficient seam allowance. This applies particularly to the shoulder, on the set of which so much depends.

When checking a block pattern, it is not necessary to do much pinning at the actual fitting, as one should be able to *visualize the necessary corrections* which can then be made *directly on the pattern*. When fitting a dress, this

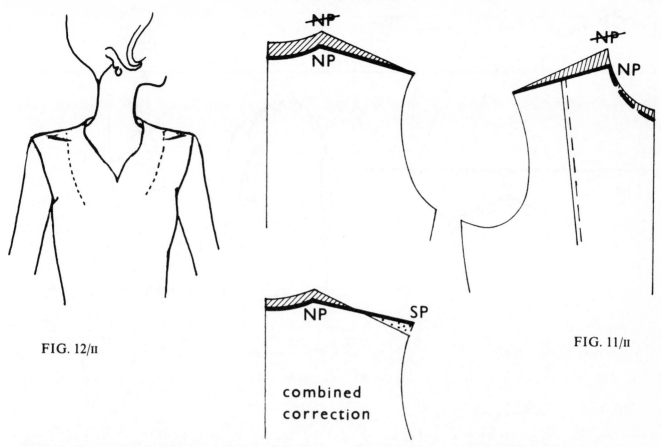

FIG. 12/II

combined
correction

FIG. 11/II

would depend on the experience and knowledge of the fitter: the more knowledgeable and familiar with pattern construction a fitter is, the less pinning and re-pinning there usually is *during* the fitting and, as a result, the less danger there is of the dress losing its original style and line.

Fashion note on square shoulders.

When square shoulders are in fashion it is usual to have a slightly higher (squarer) shoulder line in the block pattern and sometimes to make allowance in a pattern for extra shoulder padding, e.g. in coats and jackets. This fashion usually emphasizes the square shoulder defects described above: drags across the top, looseness at the neck point, etc., even on figures whose shoulders are not normally higher than average but are artificially raised by padding. At such times, therefore, these defects become more frequent.

It is necessary to point out that in some cases of bad posture and very sloping shoulders, it is considered useful **to build up the shoulder** a little, not to emphasize any 'square' effect, but just to improve its shape. Reasonably high shoulders are considered to be good shoulders as they ensure a better fit for almost any type and style of garment. Such shoulders are an asset to a professional model who has to show dresses not always made specially to fit her figure.

Uneven shoulders—a special case.

Most people have a slight difference between their right and left shoulder slopes, and in most cases this is simply ignored. However, when the defect is considered to be too noticeable or **sufficiently pronounced to affect the hang of a dress or coat**, a pad may be used to *build up* the lower shoulder or a minor correction made (such as a slight tightening of one shoulder).

Only in the case of serious unevenness would each side be fitted separately. Generally the lower shoulder would then be treated as a sloping shoulder, tightened at SP, and the armhole brought down to retain its size. In some cases it might be the higher shoulder—if unnaturally raised—that would have to be dealt with specially.

Much depends on the exact shape of the figure and, of course, on the degree of unevenness, which in some cases can amount to deformity. Such a figure, however, has generally a number of other defects as well—on one or both sides—such as a protruding shoulder blade needing a deeper dart *on one side*, or a very curved spine requiring extra back length, etc.; unusual levelling of hemline might also be needed. In such a bodice more all-over ease would probably be desirable to conceal the defects and any attempt to outline the figure too closely would probably be most unbecoming.

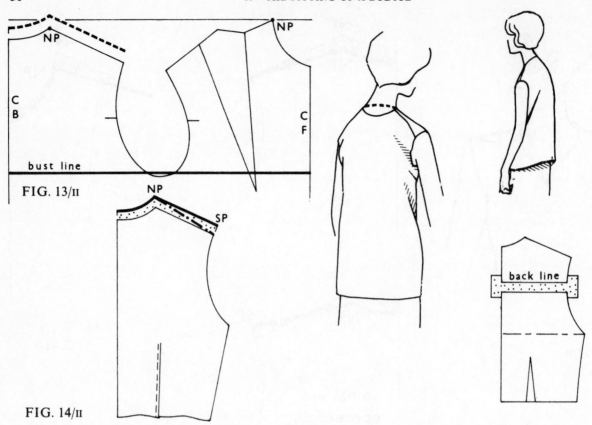

FIG. 13/II

FIG. 14/II

GROUP II—BALANCE DEFECTS

The correct balance of a bodice for each individual figure depends on the carriage of the figure, which may be **average, stooping or erect**. Balance is the right proportion between the depth of the back and the depth of the front of a bodice to suit each figure according to its shape and posture.

A simple example will make this clear: a stooping figure has a more curved, and therefore *longer*, back, and the back of the bodice, *above armhole level*, must therefore be also longer or *deeper* in proportion to the front (Fig. 13).

In an *average* bodice, with the **Front NP a little higher than the back NP**, the difference is 0·5 to just over 1 cm in the smaller sizes, increased a little (to 2 cm or more) in the larger sizes. **N.B.** In many trade patterns no difference at all is made between Back and Front height.

For a stooping figure this difference will disappear or will even be reversed (as in Fig. 13) because the back of the bodice will have to be made higher. The reverse would happen for an erect, 'short-backed' figure. When fitting, it is important to be aware of this difference and to take care *not to upset it unnecessarily* when adjusting other defects.

BALANCE OF THE BACK
BODICE BACK TOO SHORT
(not deep enough)

When the figure has a **stooping posture** (curved spine, round shoulders) and the top part of the back is therefore longer than usual, an average **bodice back is too short, i.e. not deep enough** for it. **At the fitting** it will be observed that if the back is lifted well into the neck and shoulders, it will be **too short at the CB** hem and will **stand away from the figure, with a diagonal drag from the shoulder blade** (small sketch); if the back is pulled down to its *correct waist position*—which is the right way to check the fit— it will **not quite reach up to the neck and shoulders** (big sketch). After pulling the back down just enough to make it hang straight and the crease disappear or be less pronounced, observe the fit at the top and *judge the missing height* without, however, exaggerating it (in fact it is always best to take it on the small side—this is important).

In addition to having a tendency to fall away from the neck and shoulders, the back will also tend to slip off the shoulders *dragging the seam down* and making the back armhole crease in the lower part; while *as a result of all this*, the front will be pulled up out of its correct position, and will not fit correctly either.

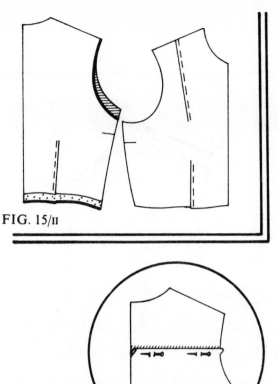

FIG. 15/II

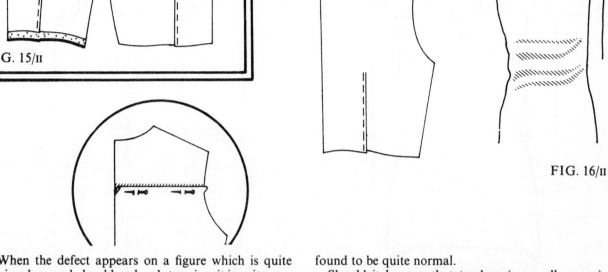

FIG. 16/II

When the defect appears on a figure which is quite obviously round-shouldered and stooping, it is quite easy to observe all this. It is, however, important not to overlook the defect on a fairly average figure, with only a *slight stoop*, i.e. when the symptoms are not very noticeable.

The correction always consists of **height addition** above the neckline and shoulders of the back (Fig. 14). The height required may only be a matter of 0·5–1 cm (which is already quite a marked balance adjustment), or more, but it may make all the difference to the set of the bodice and prevent possible trouble with sleeves later.

Correcting at a fitting is done by letting out the turnings of neckline and shoulder as much as *appears* necessary (or preferably a little less). **When correcting a pattern**, it is usual to cut across on the Back line and let in the required extra depth.

When the figure, as well as being round-shouldered, also has sloping shoulders, which happens quite often in these cases, the **height addition** is required **above neckline and NP only**, but not above SP (broken line in Fig. 14). This of course results in an increase in the slope of the shoulder and becomes **a combined correction** of balance and shoulder slope (see also Sloping shoulder—Fig. 8).

It is most important to remember that nothing should be done to the front of the bodice, *however wrong it may look*, until the back balance has been checked and corrected. When this has been done, the front may well be found to be quite normal.

Should it happen that **turnings** (seam allowance) of shoulders and neckline are **not sufficient** for the necessary letting out, then the method shown in Fig. 15 can be used: after undoing the side seam, the whole *back is moved up on the front* side seam (0·5–1 cm) to provide the *extra height above the armhole level*. This of course makes it necessary to let down the back waist (or hem) to the level of the front.

BODICE BACK TOO LONG (too deep)

When a figure has a more **erect posture** than usual and a flat or hollow back, an average **bodice back may be too long, i.e. too deep** for it. There will be either definite horizontal creases or just a general 'looseness' of the back above the waist which, *if it were to be pinned out*, would neaten it without affecting anything else except the armhole, which would be reduced. At the top—and this is important—the back fits well up to the neck and shoulders, showing *no tendency to slip back* or drag the front out of its correct position. In this case the looseness obviously indicates **excess of depth** which can be **corrected by shortening the back** (pulling it up).

At the fitting take up the back at the neckline, at NP and along the shoulder, and at SP if the armhole also appears loose (Fig. 16). A preliminary pinning out of a tuck across the back (see detail) can indicate the length

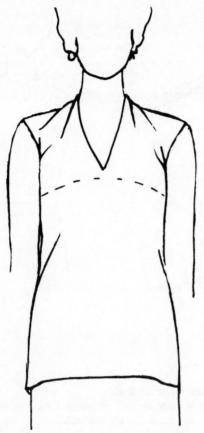

FIG. 17/II

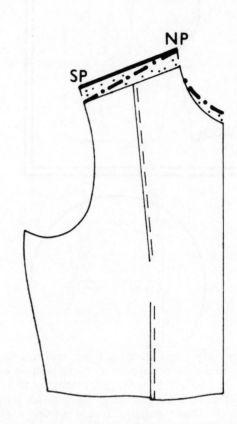

to be reduced, though it should be kept on the small side *so as not to produce the opposite defect.*

An erect figure often has square shoulders, and in such a case taking up at SP, i.e. tightening at the armhole end, is either unnecessary or wrong, since here the shoulder must remain loose. This will be achieved by **losing height at neckline and NP only** (broken line—Fig. 16) and will appear as the 'squaring' in Fig. 11.

When **correcting a pattern**, if there is *no change in the shoulder slope*, a tuck can be folded out right across (as detail).

BALANCE OF THE FRONT

BODICE FRONT TOO SHORT
(not deep enough)

For a figure with an erect posture, and either thick-set at the top or with a *higher* than usual bust, the front of an average **bodice may not have enough depth above armhole level**. Here again two cases must be considered.

A—**On a thick-set figure**, i.e. thick through the chest, top of back and shoulders, the whole shoulder section may

look constricted and actually *feel* uncomfortable. There may be a **dragging feeling round the back of the neck and at NP**, continued down into the lower part of the armhole, with short **creases** across the shoulder seam and possible tightness of armhole. As the whole front is obviously *pulled up*, this affects also the fit on the bust level from where a crease may run into the side waist. The **front clearly needs more depth above armhole level** and the defect is actually **remedied by adding height** to the top, i.e. letting out at NP, SP and the shoulder, and possibly raising the front neckline (Fig. 17). This will also increase the armhole for an over-developed Top arm.

B—On a figure with a **high bust** and an erect posture, though otherwise quite average in size or even slim, the **middle of the front may appear pulled up**. This pulling up may be slight, yet the bodice seems to lack depth between the bust level and NP. There is usually a drag from the bust down into the side seam, and the Bust Line—if it were marked as on the block—would be displaced upwards in the middle of the front.

The correction consists in **adding depth over the bust only**, i.e. letting out at NP and so bringing the Bust line down to a more normal position. The diagonal crease, if

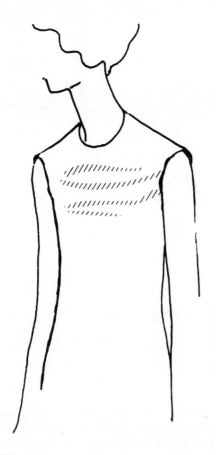

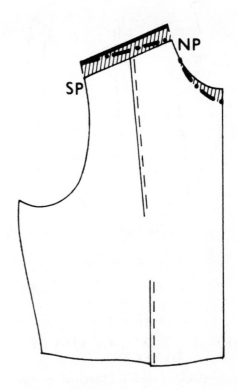

FIG. 18/II

not very deep, will usually disappear (broken line in Fig. 17. See also Fig. 8). The front neckline may need adjusting. **N.B.** It is important to bear in mind, however, that this particular defect may be *part of a bigger problem*, explained in the next section (Shape of figure defects).

A warning should be given against exaggerating the letting out at NP (where good turnings are always useful), since adding height to the front can easily bring in the opposite defect of 'Back balance too short'. Keeping the difference between the levels of front and back NP's always in mind may help to prevent this, for it is truly a matter of *'balancing' correctly the two highest points of the pattern*. When uncertain about the result, it is often a good plan to let out just 0·5 cm at a time, with a second fitting to check it, rather than risk adding too much at once and so upsetting the whole balance.

If the turnings in the shoulder seams are insufficient, e.g. for a bigger adjustment, then the same procedure can be adopted as was shown in Fig. 15; only this time it is the *front that is moved up* on the back to obtain the *extra front height* necessary at the top.

BODICE FRONT TOO LONG (too deep)

On a **flat-chested figure** the front depth of the bodice, above armhole level, may be excessive and produce **folds or looseness across the chest**—looseness which could be pinned out. **To correct** this defect the **front is shortened from the top** by taking it up at NP, SP and along the shoulder (Fig. 18), unless the shoulder end (SP) does not need tightening (broken line).

In the past, when the average posture was such that bodices generally had to be cut for more erect figures with a high bustline, patterns usually had a *bigger difference* between the highest points, and the front then was made higher than now. Most modern patterns already allow for a slight stoop (roundness of back) by placing the highest points of back and front more or less on the same level. Thus excessive height of front is less frequent, and this defect appears mainly when dealing with very flat-chested figures or those with a definite stoop. Such figures require not only an *equal balance*, but often a higher back than front.

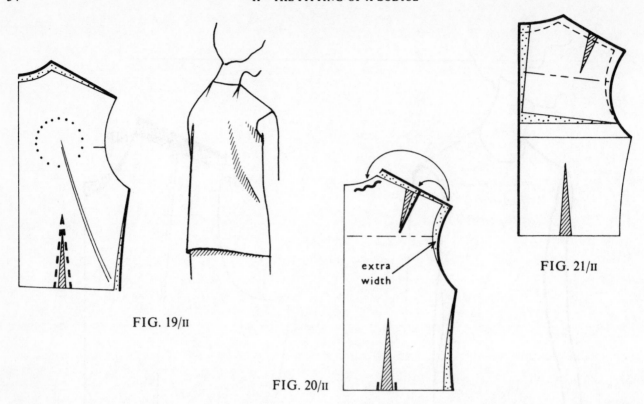

FIG. 19/II

FIG. 20/II

FIG. 21/II

extra
width

GROUP III—SHAPE OF FIGURE DEFECTS

From the fitting point of view, **the shape of the figure** is represented mainly by the **curves of the bust and shoulder-blade**, the curve of **the spine**, the prominence of **the hips** (seat and abdomen) and the **hollow of the waist**. These may be of normal shape and size or differ from the average, i.e. a figure can have a flatter or higher bust, a more prominent back curve, a thicker or smaller (pinched-in) waist, etc. It is with defects resulting from these differences that this section is concerned, though it is not always easy to isolate them completely for a basic analysis, as more often than not **they combine with the posture and shoulder defects** already explained.

PROMINENT SHOULDER BLADE
(curved spine)

A shoulder blade more prominent than usual or a curved spine will cause **a diagonal drag or long crease down to the side seam**, a **pull from the top** which may make the hem stand away at CB, possible **tightness across the back**, and usually **a loose untidy armhole**.

Since a drag or tight fold generally indicates tightness or *shortness of material between two points*, to correct this the distance between them must be lengthened. Here this can be done in two ways: **by letting out at NP** (as shown in Fig. 8), thus raising neckline, sloping the shoulder

more and altering the balance; or by **letting out at the side seam** (particularly if the seam appears overshaped) and increasing the Waist dart instead, or just leaving the back (waist and hips) looser (Fig. 19). Either of these alterations, or both combined (a little of each), would usually be sufficient to correct the defect when not very serious, i.e. just a simple diagonal crease with some pulling up of the hem. When there is also definite tightness across the top of the back, and the armhole is loose and untidy, this needs a bigger correction. The **armhole must be tightened** by smoothing its fullness up and into the shoulder seam where it is either eased or added to the dart (some of it can always be transferred to the neckline, if preferred). Since *the curve* of the shoulder blade (or spine) is more prominent, it is of course quite natural that **there is more total surplus fullness** (see Modelling Exercise I). It will be noted that moving more fullness into the shoulder not only adds to the depth of the dart, but also to the **width across the top of the back** (Fig. 20. See also Modelling Exercise VI-B, last paragraph).

It is clear from the above that a prominent shoulder blade is really a special case of 'round shoulders' and 'long back' already discussed in the previous section (Balance defects). In this case, however, usually both **extra height** and **extra width** are required to fit over the longer and wider back, as well as some **tightening of a loose edge**, i.e. of the armhole.

Fig. 21 shows a possible **complete adjustment of the**

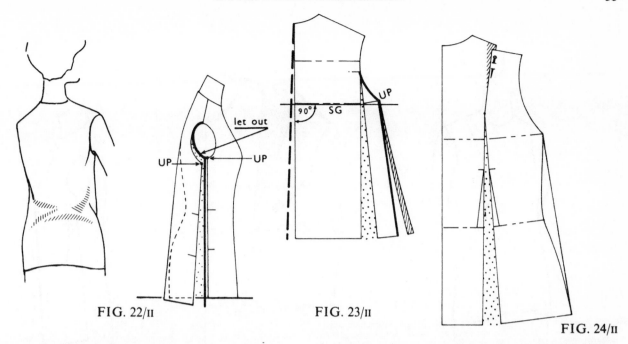

FIG. 22/II   FIG. 23/II

FIG. 24/II

pattern for this type of figure, which could be made before a fitting. Height and width are added at the same time. Slash from CB a little above the Bust line up to the armhole and, placing a sheet of paper underneath, open the slash just over 1 cm (seldom more). Re-draw the CB line from the waist, re-shape neckline and shoulder. In addition to giving width and height, this also gives a bigger slope to the shoulder and extra fullness in the neckline, from where it can be moved into the shoulder.

FIGURE WITH A PROMINENT SEAT

In smaller sizes this may be due to a bad 'sway-back' posture; in larger sizes, to over-developed hips and a very erect carriage. The bodice appears 'plastered' to the hips in the middle of the back and tends to ride up into the waist, where it forms creases *as if* the length were excessive.

When the fit is seen to be *tight all round the hips*, this is possibly the cause of the trouble, and loosening the hip width at the sides may clear it completely. When the *total hip width* appears normal, and yet **the back catches on the hips**, this may not help sufficiently, as it is not just general loosening that is required, but mainly *easing at and near the middle of the back*. The CB must, in fact, be made to detach itself from the figure and swing out a little.

To correct this defect at the fitting the side seam is opened and the whole **back moved down the front** (as in Modelling Exercise VI-A, method I). The back UP is dropped about 1 cm below the front and a new UP, *matching the front* UP, is marked higher, using the turning to build up the armhole (Fig. 22). At the same time the side seam is *sloped out a little more*: this actually *happens* if

the seam is allowed *to hang naturally* and is then marked vertically (exactly as in the Modelling exercise). As a result, the back not only gets looser on the hips, but also swings away slightly from the figure, so that it no longer catches on the hips in the middle of the back: the creases at the waist smooth out and disappear. **N.B.** A slight tightening of the hip width on *both edges* of the underarm seam may be possible later.

In a pattern the necessary adjustments can be achieved in two ways: (*a*) by adding to the hips at CB (2–2·5 cm) and taking the line up to the nape (Fig. 23); or (*b*) by slashing from the hem up to a point 8 cm up the armhole and opening the slash 4–5 cm (as Method II of Modelling Exercise VI-A). The two *alternative* adjustments of the pattern are shown on the same diagram—Fig. 23. In both cases *some of the extra width* added may possibly be lost again later on the side seam; but this must be *tested on the figure*, as generally only a small amount can be taken in before a drag develops from the shoulder blade (this varies with the figure).

When the defect is very pronounced, e.g. on a large, thick-set figure with big hips, and there is an additional pull from high (square) shoulders, the above correction, made only from the armhole, may not be sufficient and it will then be necessary to **make use of the shoulder blade dart** (or neckline fullness) by transferring part of it into the hem to ease the width on the hips. After undoing the Shoulder seam and dart, move about half of it into the armhole and then down into the side seam (exactly as in Modelling Exercise V), and finally into the hem which will thus be made to swing away more from the figure in the back. It is easier to make this correction (Fig. 24) directly on the pattern rather than at the fitting.

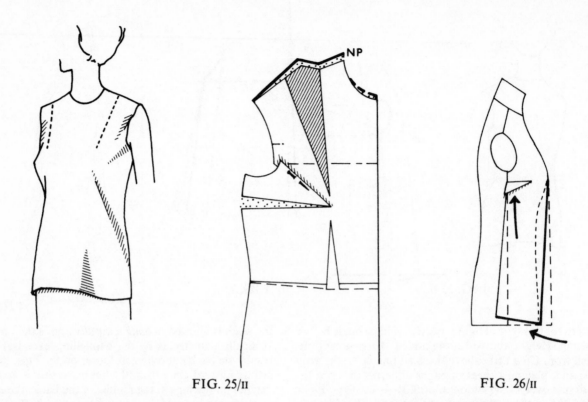

FIG. 25/II   FIG. 26/II

FIGURE WITH A PROMINENT OR HIGH BUST

A high bust may cause several defects, but the general situation is very much as with a higher shoulder blade: there is **a diagonal drag from the bust point to the side seam**, some **pulling up of the whole front from above the bust** and therefore looseness at CF hem, possible **tightness across the bust**, and nearly always **a loose, untidy armhole**.

In a **minor case** it may be quite sufficient to let out at NP (0·5–1 cm) and so drop the front exactly as explained in the previous section, where this defect is treated as a *special case of short front balance* (Fig. 17 and Fig. 8—Front).

In a **more serious case** the correction is more complicated. To clear the untidy armhole, which is a sign of *excess surplus fullness*, it is essential to **increase the depth of the Bust dart**.

At a fitting the excess armhole fullness is smoothed up into the big Shoulder dart, adding to its depth; the *new armhole* is then marked further out and the shoulder extended to its former length by using the turnings available.

Alternatively, instead of **increasing Shoulder dart**, a small **additional dart** can be used **in the underarm** after smoothing the excess fullness *down*: there must of course be sufficient seam allowance at UP to re-build the armhole higher.

If preferred, the armhole fullness can be pinned out at the fitting and this amount taken out *in the pattern* later (Fig. 25), transferring it into Shoulder or Underarm dart. The bodice would then be corrected from this pattern.

A special case must be mentioned here: it sometimes happens that with a high bust the figure is rather **hollow below the bust** so that the front here hangs away as if with extra waist width. Some of **this width can be used to increase the Bust dart**. To achieve a *more clinging fit of the front*, undo the side seam to bust level only and move the front side seam 1·5–2 cm up on the back, taking the surplus out in an underarm dart or adding it to an existing dart. This will **pull in the front under the bust** and of course add to the size of the Bust dart (Fig. 26).

In the pattern this correction appears as in Fig. 27. A dart (2·5 cm) is pinned out of the loose hem on hip level and is transferred into the underarm. The width of the pinned out dart must be replaced at the side seam to retain the original hip width. The hem will dip towards the side.

N.B. It is useful to note that an increase in the basic Bust dart can be achieved only if there is some **looseness** in the bodice **somewhere along the edge**—a loose armhole, neckline or hem which could be pinned out on the figure to mould the bodice closer to the bust, thus increasing the basic dart.

If the **diagonal crease from the Bust point** has not disappeared as a result of the other corrections (e.g.

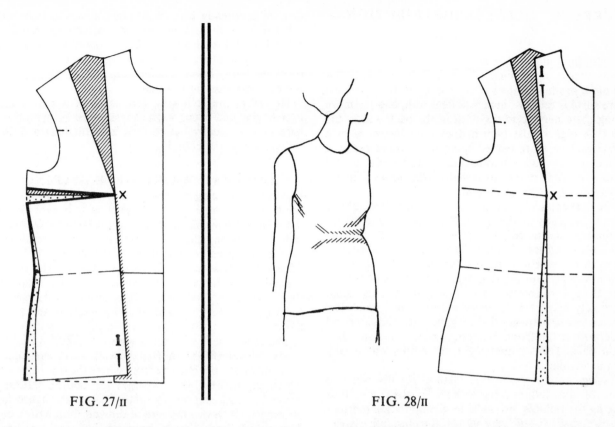

FIG. 27/II   FIG. 28/II

letting out at NP), or has not been reduced so much that it may simply be ignored, then it can be corrected only by **letting out the side seam** and increasing the Waist dart instead (as explained in Modelling Exercise VII), or accepting a *looser fit* round waist and hips (see also 'Side waist overshaping' near the end of this chapter).

Tightness across the bust can be corrected as explained earlier (Bust width re-distribution, Figs, 5, 6), though clearing the armhole by increasing the Shoulder dart would contribute to increasing the width across the bust.

FIGURE WITH A PROMINENT ABDOMEN

This is similar to the fitting of a figure with a prominent seat. In this case the front silhouette of the figure, seen sideways, does not present a straight line but **slopes out gradually below the waist**. The bodice should do the same. The defect shows mainly as CF **tightness below the waist** which produces creases above. There is also a distinct 'pull' from UP and possibly (if the shoulders are square) from SP, which does not allow the front to settle down.

In a minor case **the correction** can be made from the armhole by moving the side seam 1 cm down, exactly as was done in the back. Much more often, however, this defect is corrected by **transferring part of the shoulder dart into the hem** to make it stand away from the front of the figure.

At a fitting, after opening the side seam, part of the shoulder seam and undoing the Shoulder dart, some of the dart width (2–2·5 cm) is smoothed into the armhole and from there down the side until it finally appears in the hem (as in Modelling Exercise IX-A), where it releases the tightness over the abdomen and makes the *CF line slope out*. The Shoulder dart is pinned up smaller and the seams are re-adjusted.

In a pattern this is usually done by transferring 1·5–2·5 cm of the Shoulder dart (or more if it is thought necessary) into the hem in the usual way through the bust point (Fig. 28). **N.B.** It is of course easier to make this adjustment in the pattern and, whenever possible, this should be done in advance for this type of figure, to avoid the repinning required at the fitting.

SURPLUS FULLNESS DISTRIBUTION—

(some difficulties)

The surplus fullness caused by the curves of the figure has its own fitting problems. First of all, it is obvious that the more prominent the various curves of the figure, the more surplus fullness there is to deal with, and the more fitting there may be to do, both in the back and in the front. A higher bust (which does not always mean a bigger one), a more curved spine or shoulder blade, a smaller (more hollow) waist means **deeper darts**, and these may lead to various **technical difficulties** which a cutter/fitter has to bear in mind.

The deeper a dart is at its base, the longer it should be to run off neatly at the point. When it is short, or intentionally 'shortened', it may 'poke' (especially in some fabrics) and release fullness in the wrong place, away from the most prominent point. If stitched to its full length, it may look ugly and interfere with other lines of the design. Because of this, it is generally advisable, and often absolutely necessary, to **divide a deeper than usual dart between two or more positions**, e.g. between shoulder and underarm in the front, between shoulder and neckline in the back. This is something a cutter/fitter will usually plan in advance.

Easing, once a much used method for disposing of some of this fullness, particularly in the back, thus making the fullness 'invisible' by manipulation (shrinking, pressing), is still very useful. Surplus fullness can always be eased in the neckline, the armhole, the shoulder. This helps *to reduce the visible darts* and to keep them less deep and shorter.

When a dart is made deeper, and therefore longer, it is sometimes found that this causes *tightness where not required*, e.g. over the nape in the back neckline, or *above* and *below* the waist. A fitter must take care not to 'overfit' the darts particularly at the waist.

Different dart positions have their advantages and disadvantages, but these have already been discussed in Chapter One, in Modelling Exercise VIII.

Finally, it must be noted again that **dart manipulation** can produce **a change of silhouette**, as was clearly demonstrated when correcting 'shape of figure' defects. It is obviously necessary to take full advantage of this in fitting and to learn to use the dart fullness in such a way that the resulting outline corresponds more closely to the actual shape of the figure.

WAIST FITTING—point 14 of the Fitting Scheme. Although this can be considered as part of 'shape of figure' defects (Group III), on the whole the fit of the waist depends very much on the original **correct planning of the waist reduction** (WR) in the block. Generally, therefore, it only has **to be checked** for **tightness** and **correct position**.

Various cases of excess waist fullness or creasing have,

of course, already been mentioned in connection with other defects: these, however, were usually the result of other troubles, such as tightness on the hips *pushing the material up* into creases at the waist, etc. The waist quite often fits badly because something else in the bodice is wrong—too loose or too tight.

However, the following few cases of actual **Waist overshaping** and **wrong waist shaping** must be mentioned here as one usually has to deal with them at a fitting rather than at the planning stage.

GENERAL WAIST OVERSHAPING

Excessive **tightening of waist darts** at a fitting may disturb the fit of the whole bodice. In particular it *may tighten it too much below the waist*, so that the **bodice will tend to 'ride up'** creasing the waist and above; as a result the bodice may even become loose in the shoulders: it will appear *as if the shoulder seam needs taking in*. This defect is particularly noticeable in bodices made of stiff fabrics (heavy satins, brocade, etc.). The cause is the deepening (i.e. tightening) and consequent *lengthening* of the Waist darts.

The correct way of dealing with this defect would be to **ease the waist fit** and shorten the waist darts, particularly at and above the Hip line from where the trouble starts (when the fit here gets too tight the bodice naturally 'moves' in the direction of a smaller part of the figure, i.e. upwards). However, because of difficulties in letting out darts which have already been stitched and for other reasons also, fitters sometimes use what can only be described as an 'emergency adjustment' taking up the shoulders and so smoothing out the waist creases as much as possible by pulling them up from above.

SIDE WAIST OVERSHAPING

It has already been demonstrated in Modelling Exercise IV that the **waist will crease** and will not fit well **if pulled in too much into the side** (unless extra lengthening of side seam is possible, and the figure has a flat back). The reason for and advantage of using Waist darts, CB seam, Panel seams and even a waist join for a smoother waist fit should have become clear from the Modelling Exercises.

It sometimes happens, however, that the *theoretical distribution* of the WR between waist darts, CB seam and side seam shaping is *not quite correct for the figure*, e.g. a figure with a **very small waist**, particularly a **hollow back waist** and possibly round shoulders. There may be a drag from the shoulder blade to the side waist. The **side seam**—short or long—must be **let out at the waist** and the **Waist dart increased instead**, unless of course an altogether looser waist fit is preferred in order not to underline the curve of the back (see Fig. 19).

The same may happen in the front in the case of a high bust when, in spite of a small waist, it may be advisable

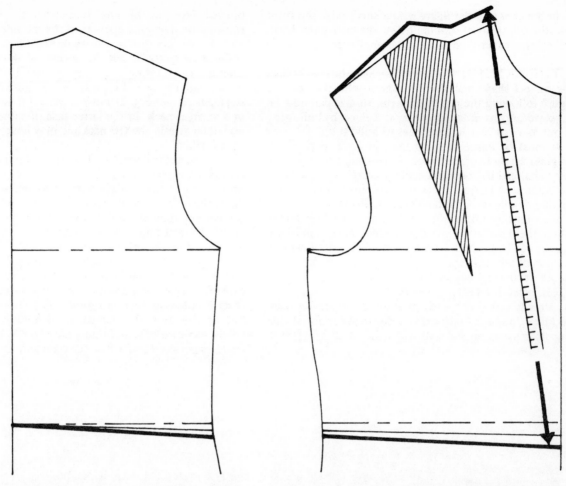

FIG. 29/II

to let out at the side seam in order to eliminate or reduce the drag from the bust. This means *increasing the waist reduction* elsewhere: in the waist dart, easing into skirt band, etc.

These defects were actually already considered when dealing with a high shoulder blade or a prominent bust (both of which increase the distance to the side waist, and so create a 'pull') but without underlining sufficiently *the part played by the fit of the waist and side seam*.

On the other hand, when a figure has **a thick waist** and a reasonably **flat back** or average shape of front, it is generally possible **to pull the bodice waist more into the side**: the waist darts then need not be so deep.

Since the above defects are connected more directly with the shape of the figure, it is usually easier to make these adjustments *at a fitting* when the exact effect can be judged.

It must be noted that a diagonal drag or crease, both on back and front, can be produced not only by the over-shaping of the waist, but also by **too much tightening of the side seam on the hips**. The same correction—letting out of seam on hip level—would apply. This means a looser fit and because of that the defect is often ignored.

The remaining points of the Fitting Scheme—waist position, final armhole and neckline shape—can be considered only after all the adjustments to the shoulder, balance and shape of figure have been made, i.e. adjustments for which it is necessary to open the shoulder seam and sometimes also the side seam.

WAISTLINE POSITION—*point 14*
Since the fitting of the waist and the correct distribution of the WR is usually done while considering the 'Shape of figure' defects, it now only remains to check **the position of the waistline on the figure**, correcting it with pins or chalk, if necessary.

On a figure with **a high bustline** it is often necessary to **drop the waistline on the CF** more than the average 1 + cm (or 2 cm in larger sizes). An additional measurement is advisable in such cases, from NP down to the front waist passing over the highest part of bust. The extra length required over an average measurement is usually found half by letting out at NP (1–2 cm) and half by a further dipping of the waist in the front. The waistline at the side is then taken a little lower than usual, and finally run into the CB at the original level (Fig. 29).

In the case of **a flat figure** with a small bust, the front waistline, instead of dipping below the horizontal level, either runs exactly on it, or sometimes even rises *above* it.

THE ARMHOLE—*point 15*—can be finally **checked for correct shape and size**. Outline it with pins on the figure following the top of the arm. Its size can now be adjusted only by *dropping or raising UP*, i.e. by hollowing it out more or by using turnings to build it up.

It must be borne in mind that, however correct the original armhole of the block, at this stage it may have been changed by the various other corrections made on the bodice, and a final checking is therefore essential (for further details see Chapter Three on Sleeves).

Care must be taken when outlining the armhole on the top of the shoulder to give the **shoulder line its full length** as required by the figure, unless one is following a definite fashion of setting in the sleeve higher or lower than usual (more details in Chapter Three).

THE NECKLINE—*point 16*.

As already stated in the explanations given for the **Back neckline**—point 2—any *extra width* required for it (see Fig. 1) must be introduced when the shoulder seam is opened. Now, at this final stage when the various corrections involving the opening of the shoulder seam have already been completed, **the whole neckline** can at last be **outlined correctly to suit the posture of the figure**. This usually means cutting it out more on the CF while keeping it very high on the CB for a stooping figure or a **forward sloping neck** (see Fig. 2) and vice versa for an erect figure or a **straight neck**. In the latter case, if some letting out was done at NP, the CF neckline may have to be raised even further.

It will be easily understood why these final adjustments cannot be carried out earlier, i.e. before the more important corrections of shoulder, balance and shape of figure have been dealt with. They seldom, however, present any difficulty and in case of any doubt they can always be tested again at another fitting, without in any way upsetting the other corrections.

This completes the Fitting Scheme as applied to a basic bodice, whether a block or the bodice of a dress. In the case of a garment there would, of course, be **various points of style, fashion and becomingness** to be considered as well; but, as already said, for these no definite rules or even advice can be given, and fitters have to rely on common sense, experience and a flair for style and fashion.

A correct fit of a sleeve is not due entirely to a good cut or to the shape of the sleeve itself, or even to the right way of setting it into the armhole. There are other factors, connected mainly with the bodice fit, which play an important part in sleeve fitting. It is therefore useful to discuss some of these before dealing with actual sleeve defects.

EFFECT OF MEASUREMENTS AND FIT OF BODICE ON SLEEVE FITTING

Apart from the measurements of the sleeve and of the finally shaped armhole, **the measurements of the bodice** may have an effect on the shape of the armhole and, through this, on the fit of the sleeve.

The Bust measurement is important because it affects **the size of the armhole** across. In the theoretical study of the Bodice block* it is explained that the size of the **armhole depends on its depth, its height and its width** (Fig. 1). If the bodice is not reasonably *wide under the arm*, the armhole may not have sufficient *width* and it will then be necessary to make it *deeper* in order *to achieve the right size*. Since cutting it *down* shortens the bodice underarm, this, in certain circumstances, can make the sleeve uncomfortable: the sleeve will pull when the arm is raised (see 'Defects' lower). Thus, a close fitting bodice

* *Dress Pattern Designing*—Chapter Two.

with sleeves, for instance, if taken in too much under the arm, may make sleeve fitting difficult.

Back, Chest and Shoulder measurements. When, at the end of the bodice fitting, the armhole outline is verified, the Back, Chest and Shoulder measurements are *checked* at the same time: a correct armhole finally determines these measurements, even though an experienced fitter may already be visualizing the type of armhole 'in fashion' when first taking them. All these measurements can in fact be taken bigger or smaller according to *the shape of the armhole required by the style* and by *the set of the sleeve* aimed at.

The *basic* measurements are obtained by just following the edge of the shoulder bone and the natural armscye ('arm's eye'). For a lower 'off-the-shoulder' sleeve set they would tend to be slightly increased; for a 'high-on-the-shoulder' sleeve set—reduced (see 'Fashion silhouette of the shoulder' lower).

Defects in the fit of the bodice can also influence the fit of a sleeve, and it is most important not to overlook them. For instance, a wrong shoulder slant, i.e. tightness or looseness at the armhole end makes it more difficult to achieve a neat fit of the sleeve. This, however, would generally be corrected at an earlier stage.

There is, of course, some danger that when such a defect is not very pronounced, it may be overlooked or even

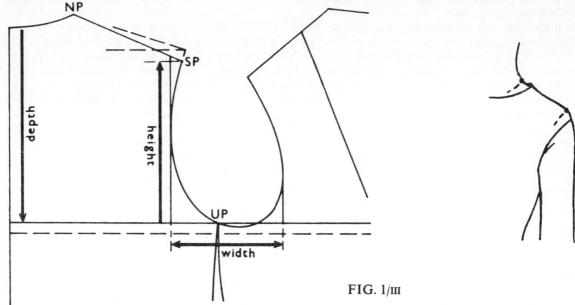

FIG. 1/III

41

misunderstood. One particular case should be mentioned, precisely because it is not always understood correctly: **tightness of armhole over the shoulder bone** (i.e. at SP) may sometimes *drag the armhole down the top of the arm*, so that the shoulder *appears* to be too long. There is a temptation *to shorten it* at the final outlining of the armhole, and so to fit the sleeve higher on the shoulder than necessary. In actual fact the length is probably quite correct if it were not for the tendency of the shoulder to pull away from the neck and down the arm as the result of the *tightness at SP* (sketch). Once this pull is removed by easing at SP, the shoulder will regain its normal position, permitting the armhole to be marked correctly. **N.B.** This is something which happens fairly often when the sleeve is tacked into the armhole before a first fitting, when *the thickness of the untrimmed turnings* may be the *cause of the 'tightness'* at SP: once they are trimmed and pressed flat, the pull disappears. Because of this it is not generally advisable to tack in a sleeve before the shoulder tightness has been checked on the figure.

The width of the back neckline, if wrong, may also affect the armhole and sleeve. As already stated in Chapter Two (point 2), when the neckline is too wide it *displaces* the shoulder seam, allowing it to slip over the shoulder bone on to the top of the arm. Here again the shoulder is not too long—it is just *pushed out* beyond its correct position. Its length, therefore, should not be reduced until the back neckline has been checked and made to fit correctly.

A correct bodice balance is also essential for a good armhole and sleeve fit. When **the back balance is too short**, the armhole does not set firmly on the shoulder and tends to slip back, dragging the front armhole out of its correct position over the shoulder bone. When **the front balance is too short** the front armhole may be tight in the hollow near the Chest level (see Balance defects—Chapter Two). However, these defects are clearly visible at an early stage of the fitting and would not generally be overlooked. Even more does this apply to *excess* of front or back balance which is seldom left uncorrected. Once the balance is corrected, the armhole regains its normal position and can then be outlined to follow the shape of the shoulder. Thus, so long as the armhole is 'unsettled', for whatever reason, no sleeve fitting can be reliable.

Finally, **shape of figure defects** undoubtedly affect the armhole and sleeve. In the case of a **figure with a prominent bust** or **an over-developed shoulder blade**, the armhole will always be looser and more untidy than on an average figure. In both cases, however, the untidy armhole is a symptom of a trouble which should have been dealt with before the sleeve fitting stage is reached.

Thus all the bodice defects mentioned above may influence the final appearance of a sleeve; but as they would usually be corrected before the sleeve is set in, there is no need to do more than note their relevance to sleeve fitting.

THE ARMHOLE—ITS FIT, SHAPE AND SIZE

The average fit of an armhole can be described as fairly close, i.e. neatly clinging to the shoulder bone, but without being too tight, particularly in the lower part.

Tightness of armhole, as a defect, occurs mainly on large figures with overdeveloped shoulder and chest muscles, or fat round the top arm. Since—as was shown in several Modelling exercises (I, II, VII)—a sufficiently close fit is due largely to the armhole being pulled up by the shoulder darts (front and back), it is obvious that when the armhole is so tight that it 'cuts' into the figure, the darts may have to be reduced *to release a little width* into the armhole (Fig. 2). This shows that increasing the *shoulder* dart, particularly in the front, has its limits, even if it appears to be necessary for other reasons. It is in such cases that an *additional underarm dart*, to increase bust shaping, can be so useful.

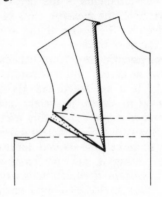

FIG. 2/III

Looseness of the armhole. When all the necessary *adjustments of the bodice*, which have the effect of neatening the armhole, have been completed, and the armhole still appears loose and flutes at the edge, there are ways of *tightening it by manipulation*. It can be eased and shrunk, or tightened on a tape or strip of lining material to make it cling better, for instance in the back, near the curve of a prominent shoulder blade. Padding of the shoulder is also helpful since it clears untidy fullness by *pulling up* the armhole. It is much used for this purpose when 'square' shoulders are in fashion, but also at all times for difficult figures with sloping or *uneven* shoulders (such building up of a sloping shoulder need not necessarily emphasize 'squareness'). All this manipulation belongs to the making-up technique, but would be borne in mind by a fitter.

A certain amount of tightness may always be caused by **armhole turnings** (seam allowance) which, as already, mentioned, may even pull the armhole out of its correct position. A fitter must be aware of this difficulty and, whenever necessary, cut into any *extra wide turnings*, though very carefully, leaving at least 2·5 cm beyond the fitting line (possibly more in easily fraying materials).

The shape of the armhole varies according to the figure and garment and *will not always be necessarily as on the Block pattern*. It can be said that the shape is affected by:

(*a*) The size and proportions of the figure
(*b*) The shape and posture of the figure
(*c*) The style or type of garment
(*d*) The influence of fashion.

Thus a person with a wide Back and Chest measurement *in proportion to the Bust* will have a *narrower armhole* (Fig. 3) because of the smaller *total bust width* available in the pattern. If it cannot be extended up-

well exposed and either very high (and even 'square') under the arm or, on the contrary, quite low.

The important **influence of fashion** both on the set of the sleeve and on the resulting shape of armhole must now be discussed in greater detail.

The fashion silhouette of the shoulders (or 'Fashion shoulder line') is the effect produced by the sleeve joining the bodice in a particular way. This coming together of sleeve and armhole may be along the basic or natural armhole line (sketch a). From time to time, however, the shoulder line changes to follow a different 'fashion

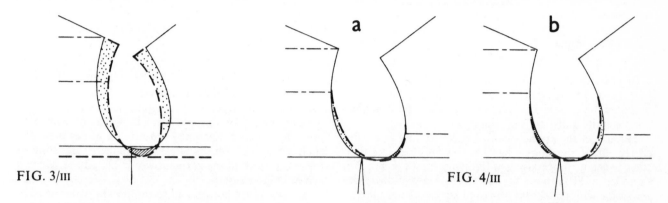

FIG. 3/III   FIG. 4/III

wards, because no squaring of the shoulder is required, it will have to come lower down the side seam to obtain sufficient size.

The shape also changes slightly with **the posture** of the figure. **When the figure is stooping**, the shoulder is in a forward position and the armhole must usually be kept high, i.e. filled out in the back hollow and cut out more in the front hollow where the muscle presses on it (Fig. 4-a). Conversely, **when the figure is erect**, the armhole often needs cutting out more in the back and filling out in the front, near the Chest point (Fig. 4-b), where otherwise there may be a gap.

There are also some **styles which influence the shape** of the armhole. Thus for *sleeveless dresses* it is often made to come over the shoulder beyond the usual chest and back width; though, on the other hand, fashion may dictate a completely different outline, with the shoulder

silhouette' and with it changes the setting in of the sleeves and the armhole.

Thus, fashion may favour a slightly *sloping shoulder* line achieved by lengthening shoulder and widening back and chest to produce *an off-the-shoulder effect* reminiscent of the Kimono cut (sketch b). This usually requires a lowering of the narrower armhole below UP, as without it one cannot achieve the right size.

The sleeve may also be set high on the shoulder for a **narrow shoulder effect**, with or without raising of the underarm at UP (Fig. 5 and sketch c). Or it may be set into a 'squared' and extended shoulder which is built up and padded to produce a **wide and square shoulder effect** (Fig. 6 and sketch d). In each case the shoulder, the back and the chest measurements are adjusted accordingly, and so the armhole changes its shape.

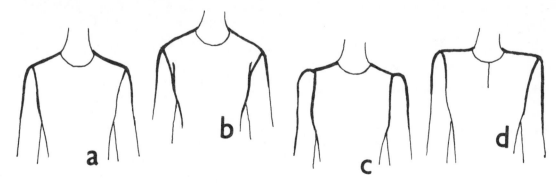

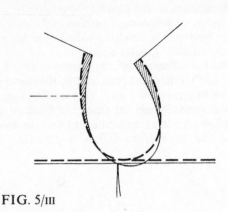

FIG. 5/III

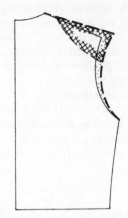

FIG. 6/III

In most cases the difference in the pattern from the *basic* set and fit is small; but the general effect of sleeves mounted high on the shoulder or just below the shoulder bone is quite a distinctive fashion feature.

The size of the armhole can be checked only after the correct fit of the bodice has been established. At this stage, when no more easing or tightening at the end of the shoulder (at SP) is possible, nor any increase or decrease across the width *under the arm* or at back and chest level, the armhole can be adjusted to its final size only by lowering it at UP, i.e. by **increasing its depth**.

This presents, of course, a certain danger—that of unduly shortening the bodice underarm and so producing a 'pull' on the sleeve when the arm is raised. The defect is much more likely and more noticeable in 'waisted' or belted dresses, where the waistline does not move easily with the raising of the arm as it does in loose hanging styles. As a basic principle, therefore, the armhole should be cut *down* as little as possible. **N.B.** It is useful to point out here that an *uncomfortable* armhole is sometimes due *not to a small size*, but to a *wrong shape* (e.g. not cut out enough in the front for a stooping figure), or just to big turnings before they are trimmed and pressed.

As an extra precaution against excessive cutting down of armholes, as well as against leaving them too small, it is very useful to have an idea of what **a correct armhole size for each figure** should be.

Some fitters know what a suitable armhole would be from long experience; some follow a chart of average sizes; some prefer to take an actual measurement on the figure. It is also possible to work out a reasonably accurate size by taking a *proportion of an individual measurement*,

such as bust or top arm. The proportion of TA plus 12–13 cm for a **minimum armhole** (or 14 cm, sometimes even more in larger sizes) is quite a useful 'Checking measurement' for this purpose. It would of course be more for garments actually requiring a looser armhole, such as blouses, overalls, jackets (in all these cases some of the extra width of the garment would already provide an armhole increase).

When it is not convenient to outline the armhole fully on the figure or dangerous to cut into it as much as finally required, one can outline the upper part only, down to B and F, then undo the top of the side seam, enough to allow the armhole *to set correctly, without any underarm strain*, and mark with a pin what appears to be a suitable level for the underarm point (UP). Working from this one can complete the armhole on the flat, referring to the 'checking measurement', which is of particular value in cases when one has to work away from the figure.

There are, of course, various **reasons why an armhole may have to be cut down lower**: it may have to be done to suit a special style or type of garment requiring extra armhole ease; or for a garment worn *over another*, such as a jacket, coat, or overall; or to follow the *shape of the figure*, as when the whole armhole is moved to a lower level because of sloping shoulders; or for reasons of fashion requiring an 'off-the-shoulder' sleeve set; or because of a 'narrowing' of the armhole, e.g. to cover the shoulder bone well in a sleeveless dress; or sometimes simply to comply with personal preference for low-cut armholes. In every case the danger of affecting the underarm fit of the whole garment must be borne in mind (see 'Defects' lower).

THE SLEEVE—ITS CONSTRUCTION AND CORRECT HANG

THE CONSTRUCTION (pattern analysis)

The sleeve is drafted with a certain depth of crown above DC (depth of crown) line. When set into *a basic armhole* it must give a correct fit over **the angle formed by the shoulder and the arm**. There is thus an obvious connection between **the depth of the sleeve crown (T–DC)** and **the shoulder (NP–SP)**. The **combined length** NP–SP plus T–DC

in one particular way, it is not always easy to establish **the best depth of the crown** for average use or even for a particular figure. This explains why in bespoke dressmaking *individual* sleeve fitting is necessary and why the depth of the crown so often needs adjusting.

Another important factor in the construction of a sleeve is its **underarm length** which is closely connected with the depth of the crown. Assuming that *the total length* of the sleeve is constant, then, when the depth of the crown (or the head) is deeper, the sleeve underarm

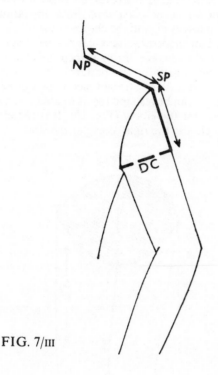

FIG. 7/III

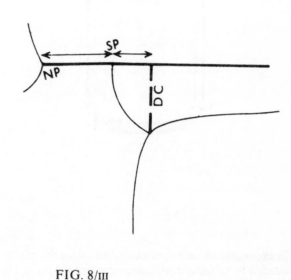

FIG. 8/III

(Fig. 7) must be sufficient (but not too long) to enable the sleeve to hang correctly.

If the combined length is *too short*, the sleeve will pull from the top and there will be drags from the shoulder point (see 'Defects' lower) when the arm is at rest i.e. down; though with the arm raised it may fit quite well because of the shorter distance (Fig. 8). If it is *too long*, it may fit well when the arm is right down, but will be less comfortable with any upward or forward movement of the arm. However, since the *shoulder length is already fixed* by the requirements of the figure (or style, or fashion), the necessary hang of the sleeve can *at this stage* be obtained only by a **change in the depth of the crown**.

As the arm must move and take up various positions in relation to the body, while the sleeve can be set in only

seam will be shorter, and vice versa (Fig. 9). One cannot always easily establish the best relation between crown and length of seam, as various considerations may enter into it. Broadly speaking, where *appearance of the sleeve is more important than comfort* (e.g. in many tailored garments), the crown is usually made deeper; where *comfort is the main consideration* (e.g. in sport clothes or in clothing used specially for work involving arm movement) a *longer underarm*, and therefore a shorter crown, are generally the rule.

From all this it will be seen that it is difficult to give a perfect crown, once and for all, to fit all figures. Even the crown for an individual figure may undergo various slight changes to adapt it to a *big variety of garments and styles*, to say nothing of the constant changes in fashion.

is neutralized by a corresponding lowering of the under-arm point (U), so that the final crown remains much the same as the basic, but is placed lower down the arm.

The shape of the figure can also affect the height of the crown. For instance, those **with a square shoulder** will need a **higher crown** (more length from NP–SP to DC), **a sloping shoulder**—generally **a lower (shorter) crown**. A **big Top arm muscle** may require more *height* as well as *width* in the head of the sleeve. Most of this is established mainly at the fitting.

Another important point in the construction of the pattern is **the provision for elbow bending**. It matters particularly in long, tight sleeves; and also in *styles which must follow the curve of the arm*. Both appearance and comfort are involved, and the choice of the block pattern is decisive: an incorrect sleeve cannot be shaped satisfactorily *on the arm* at a fitting (except by a very skilled fitter able to transform the pattern). It is useless, for instance, to fit a plain Straight sleeve as a close fitting style, unless it can be reshaped so as to obtain some curve and fullness for the elbow (Fig. 10). It is therefore important to choose the right sleeve at the start.

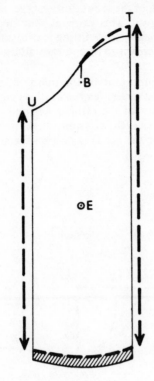

FIG. 9/III

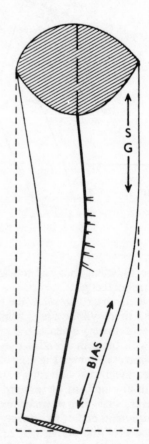

FIG. 10/III

The average basic sleeve crown, as drafted for the block, is intended to fit fairly high under the arm (at point U) and just to reach the shoulder bone at the top (point T). In a sleeve block it is generally advisable to keep the underarm seam at its longest (and most comfortable) consistent with a neat appearance of the sleeve at the top. It is not advisable to make the basic crown deeper than is absolutely necessary because of possible difficulties that may arise when the basic sleeve is used for various adaptations (e.g. the Kimono construction). The basic crown, however, will often be changed in depth for various purposes and for reasons of fashion, and should not be treated as a final, permanent crown.

The fashion aspect of the sleeve setting must again be referred to. When it is fashionable for the sleeve to be set *high* on the shoulder, this usually means a higher crown; and where there is a particular emphasis on a **'squared' effect**, there will always be a definite and often **considerable addition above the normal crown** in a 'fashion sleeve' pattern. When the sleeve must be set in **below the shoulder bone**, this usually means a lowering of the crown; though in some cases (depending on style and other details) this

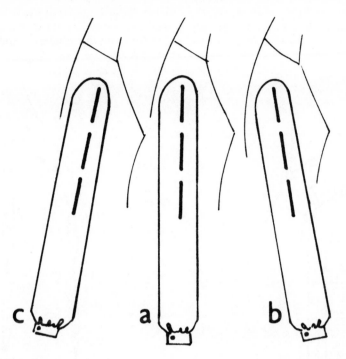

FIG. 11/III

THE HANG OF THE SLEEVE

A sleeve should hang **straight down** in a vertical line (Fig. 11-a) or with a **slight forward swing** (Fig. 11-b). A swing to the back (Fig. 11-c) should be avoided.

When the sleeve hangs straight down, the fit on the back line (or hindarm) is usually neater, i.e. more pulled up; but it may be a little less comfortable when the arm is moved forward. When the sleeve is set to swing slightly forward, the fit is more comfortable for arm movement, but there may be some unavoidable slight creasing or fullness in the back when the arm is held straight down. This is a matter for the fitter's decision; but, generally speaking, a straight hang is more usual in dressmaking (except for special purpose garments), while the 'forward' swing is used more in tailoring (particularly men's tailoring).

The sleeve is set into the armhole usually by **matching one or more Inset points**, such as points B and F, or forearm and hindarm pitch (in tailoring). Many fitters, mainly dressmakers, balance a sleeve from one point of contact only—**the highest point of the sleeve crown matching the highest point of the shoulder**; they then pull up the forearm and hindarm folds until they are quite taut and the middle of the sleeve hangs straight down the Top arm (the arm must be held in a natural position down the body). **A correctly balanced sleeve** has the SG running in a *vertical line down the arm* and the X–SG in a *horizontal line across the top* of the sleeve (Fig. 12).

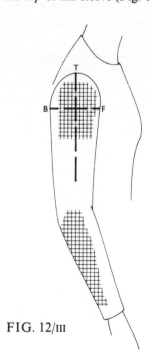

FIG. 12/III

The pinning of a sleeve on the stand to ascertain its hang provides a very useful preliminary fitting exercise and on the whole is much used by fitters for checking purposes both before and after a fitting (experienced fitters know

If, **as an experiment**, the excess fullness is smoothed *down the armhole* both ways, to get a perfectly *flat top*, it will soon be observed that creases and folds appear down the forearm and hindarm, and the sleeve loses its neat,

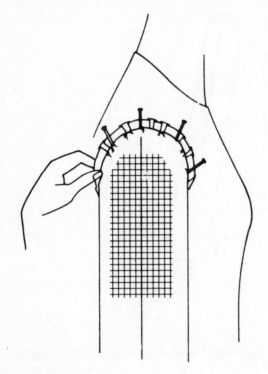

FIG. 13/III

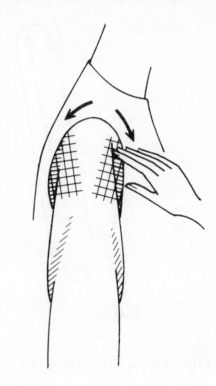

FIG. 14/III

of course exactly what a correctly hanging sleeve should look like).

The sleeve is pinned with its highest point (point T) to the highest point of the armhole: on the figure this is usually at or near the shoulder seam, *depending on the actual position of the seam* (in the middle or slightly back) and also on *the shape of the shoulder* (a forward sloping shoulder may have its highest point 0·5–1 cm or even more to the front of the seam). On the stand the *middle* of the shoulder is taken as the highest point. Pull up the forearm and hindarm of the sleeve (points F and B) and pin them to the 'armhole' of the stand (or to a bodice armhole), approximately 9–10 cm to the front and back of the top point. Distribute the excess length of the crown as shown in Fig. 13 allowing more for the front.

The exercise not only demonstrates the correct hang of a sleeve, but also shows convincingly that to achieve it there must always be **some surplus fullness over the curve** of the shoulder, *if the forearm and hindarm folds are to be sufficiently pulled up.*

pulled-up appearance (Fig. 14). The X–SG *sags at both ends* and it is not possible to get rid of the creases except by pulling sleeve up again.

The crown surplus fullness (which of course is a 'dart' developing over the 'angle' of the shoulder) varies according to the height of the crown, which in turn depends on the way the sleeve is set in, and on the shape of the figure. The higher the set of the sleeves, and the squarer (higher) the shoulder, the more fullness there will always be to deal with.

Although at the pattern making stage the marking of B and F on the armhole is a convenient device, it must be understood that *from a fitting point of view* it is of course guesswork, as is also the amount of ease allowed in the crown of a basic sleeve pattern (2–2·5 cm is an approximate quantity based on a moderate depth of crown). As already explained, many people need, or prefer, a higher crown and so will usually have more ease to deal with. When a fitting is possible, it is more practical to make a more cautious estimate of crown depth and ease in the pattern, increasing it at the fitting, *if necessary.*

The main thing to understand is that in themselves points B and F *on the armhole* of a bodice do not guarantee a correct hang of the sleeve on the figure. Once checked, however, they can usually be relied upon to give the right balance in further patterns, though results may vary occasionally. In every case **points B and F on the armhole are correct only when the sleeve hangs correctly**, as shown in Fig. 13.

One other point which it is useful to mention at this stage is that neither the **shoulder seam** of the bodice nor its **underarm seam** can be relied upon to determine the position of the sleeve in the armhole, for the simple reason that their position may change in a pattern and does not always come in exactly the same place on the figure. Still, for practical purposes fitters do use them when setting in a sleeve: they know they can always adjust it at the fitting.

Thus, whatever the purely practical methods adopted by different fitters, what actually matters is *to establish a correct hang of the sleeve on the figure* and not just to follow a rigid matching of points on sleeve and armhole.

SETTING IN A SLEEVE

Before setting in a sleeve into an armhole, it is advisable to **measure round the top of the sleeve** as accurately as possible (with tape measure held on edge) and to **compare this with the size of the armhole**, to see what the excess fullness is likely to be.

In an average case the top part of the armhole can easily absorb up to 2·5 cm, and with suitable fabrics, even more. When the fullness exceeds 4 cm (or the fabric is unsuitable), some difficulty in disposing of it by the usual method of pressing and shrinking may be experienced. Several things are then possible: (*a*) to reduce (flatten) the crown to shorten the outer edge which, however, would be suitable only for some garments and styles (shirts, some blouses, overalls, etc.); (*b*) to tighten the whole sleeve on the underarm seam, suitable of course only for really close fitting styles; (*c*) to increase the top part of the armhole between B and F by 'squaring' the shoulder (when padding is acceptable a small pad would take care of the resulting looseness); (*d*) to increase the size of the armhole *downwards* (the dangers of this have been explained, but it is often done). The most usual, however, for an experienced and skilled fitter is *to manipulate the setting in* by easing and shrinking and so to work in the excess until a smooth fit, without any *visible* fullness is achieved. Much trouble in sleeve fitting and finishing comes from a lack of this skill which only practice and experience can give.

To complete the setting in of the sleeve, check the fit of the lower part to see how it goes into the armhole. Normally the lower part of the sleeve head—below B and F—should go in quite flat, though there are exceptions to this. However, it is possible that it may be too big or too small for the remaining part of the armhole.

When the sleeve is *too big for the lower armhole*, points

B and F can be moved a little higher on the bodice: this must however be done *equally on both sides*, so as not to upset the balance of the sleeve. This will of course add a little to the fullness at the top, but the amount is usually small. As already mentioned, it is also possible to increase the armhole slightly *downwards*, provided the bodice side seam is not getting too short. Hollowing it out more in the front may also help in some cases.

Finally, one can ease some of the extra sleeve width in the lower part, and this may even be advisable in some cases (e.g. for an extra big or fat top arm). It is quite possible to get rid of a *small amount* of ease in the lower part to avoid increasing the armhole.

When the *sleeve is too small for the lower armhole*, and it is not considered desirable or possible to widen it by letting it out on the underarm seam, B and F on the armhole can be brought down a little, but absolutely equally on both sides, so that the balance is not affected: this should be *checked on the stand*. Again the amount involved can only be very small, unless the **sleeve itself is the wrong size** and thus is **basically wrong for the armhole**.

N.B. It may be useful to emphasize at this stage that it is not sufficient to have a correct size of armhole *in the pattern*, or even to achieve it at the fitting: it must be possible *to keep it to this size* throughout work on the garment. Armholes tend *to stretch* and are often too big by the time the sleeve has to go in: this must be kept in mind and *suitable precautions taken*. Sometimes an armhole—if too big—may simply need tightening by 'pulling up' to reduce its size (this, of course, is not a problem of the wholesale manufacturing trade).

The underarm seam of the sleeve must also be checked to see that *it does not come to the back of the bodice seam*, for this makes a sleeve *uncomfortable in wear*. This applies particularly to the really **tight sleeves** which **in wear tend to 'twist'** *back* round the elbow and *forward* at the wrist. This twisting cannot be avoided, but allowance is made for it in the pattern construction (Fig. 15): the underarm seam, forming a 'bulge' on the back edge, is brought *forward on the arm* to prevent it catching on the elbow point. For the same reason the whole seam of a tight sleeve is placed more forward in the armhole than the seam of a straight loose sleeve: the latter in some cases may even match the bodice seam, or be only slightly to the front of it.

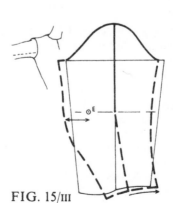

FIG. 15/III

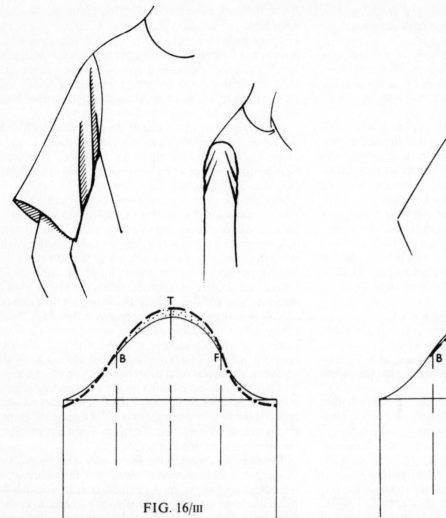

FIG. 16/III   FIG. 17/III

Having considered at some length the construction of the sleeve and armhole in their relation to the problems of sleeve fitting, it is now necessary to give examples of **defects in sleeves which are due mainly to variations in the shape and posture of the figure.**

A—DEPTH OF CROWN DEFECTS

Crown too low or too shallow. When the crown of the sleeve is too flat (shallow), so that it makes the combined shoulder and sleeve top length (NP–SP–T–DC) **too short over the shoulder bone**, there is a **pull from the top** of the shoulder and **diagonal creases** run usually in both directions (sketch–Fig. 16). In the case of a short sleeve, the front lower edge tends to stand away from the arm. If the pull is considerable, it will affect the underarm, producing there what *looks* like excess fullness.

When the defect is slight, showing mainly on the top, **letting out the crown at point T** usually clears it (Fig. 16). But, if there is not enough seam allowance at point T,

it is often necessary to *pull up the underarm* as well. In both cases the result is, of course, the same—**increasing or deepening of the crown** between T and DC level, with a corresponding **reduction in the length of the underarm** of the sleeve (Fig. 9). Although the sleeve length can always be adjusted at the wrist, this would increase the *total* length which is probably not required. In choosing the method, the fitter will be guided by turnings available, the overall sleeve length and also by the requirements of comfort in wear.

There are various **reasons why a crown can be too shallow**: the shoulder may be more square or the shoulder bone more prominent than usual, or the arm may have an overdeveloped muscle; the *shoulder seam of the bodice may be too short*, in which case the correction must be made wholly or partly on the bodice; or it may happen for reasons of fashion, e.g. when the shoulder must be 'squared' and padded; or when, irrespective of fashion, a 'built-up' shoulder is used to ensure a better fit (e.g. on a figure with very sloping shoulders).

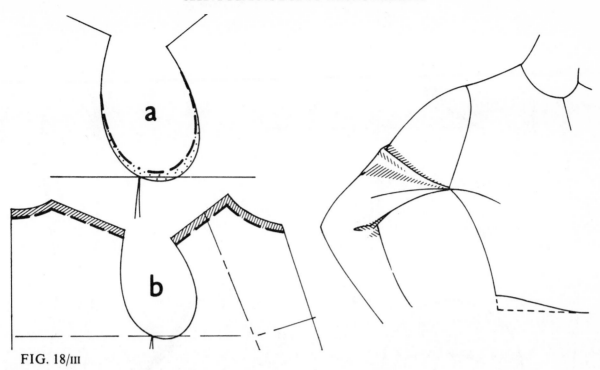

FIG. 18/III

Crown too high or too deep. This is the opposite defect which is caused by the crown depth between T and DC being excessive. It may show itself in several different ways, according to the width and type of sleeve (loose, tight, tailored). It is generally quite *obvious* that there is too much length above the DC line and the excess may form one or more **horizontal creases** which tighten and **press on the top arm** when the arm is raised or moved forward even slightly (sketch-Fig. 17). However, because the fit of the sleeve *when the arm is down* often appears to be satisfactory, the defect does not always attract attention. It is for the fitter to assess the situation and to decide whether it must be dealt with, always bearing in mind that sleeves with excessively high, and therefore narrow, crowns tend to tear out of the armhole in wear.

To correct reduce the crown height by taking the sleeve up at the top (Fig. 17), gradually running the new line into the old one. The length of the sleeve lost at the top is added at the wrist, thus increasing the underarm length.

B—SLEEVE DEFECTS DUE TO WRONG ARMHOLE

Armhole too deep. This can be a very serious defect, often involving quite a big alteration. It happens when the armhole is enlarged by cutting it down too much on the bodice side seam. The whole garment pulls up when the arm is moved, with tight folds forming across the sleeve top (sketch-Fig. 18). The sleeve feels most uncomfortable and movement restricting.

Diagram 'a' of Fig. 18 shows the necessary correction, i.e. the **raising of the armhole** to a higher level; but when,

as often happens, there is not enough seam allowance to do so, the only possibility of getting out of this difficulty is to re-cut the whole top of the bodice by taking it up at the shoulders (Diagram 'b'-Fig. 18). This may or may not be possible, and is in any case a complicated alteration. Therefore, whenever armhole size is increased *downwards*, the length of the side seam must be watched carefully and not allowed to be shortened to the point when a sleeve pinned to it will pull (test by raising arm).

It must be added that the defect, if not excessive, is sometimes overlooked in loose hanging dresses and coats, as with the raising of the arm the whole garment moves up quite freely and then falls back into its place. The situation is quite different, however, when the bodice is more or less *fixed* at the waist, either by a tight belt or by a tight fit of the waist itself. As with the previous defect, there is a danger of the sleeve tearing away from the armhole or wearing out in the lower part.

Armhole too small is hardly a defect since it can always be made bigger. Yet, there is at least one case where this may lead to further fitting complications: **once the sleeve is set in and finished off**, a tight armhole is *not quite so easy to correct*. There may be difficulties in adapting the sleeve to the larger armhole if its wrist is already finished off and all the turnings are trimmed (e.g. the sleeve may pull on the underarm as a result of a re-adjustment).

It is particularly in cases when a final fitting is impossible, or when there is reluctance to snip too much into the turning of the armhole at the fitting, that it is so important *to know theoretically* what a *suitable armhole for each figure* should measure.

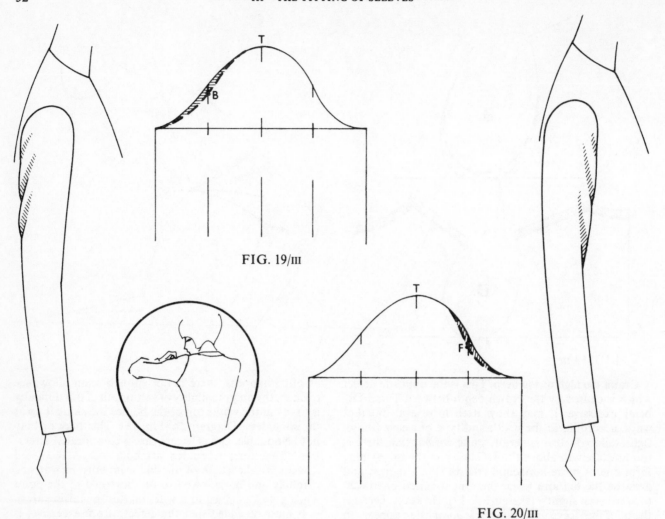

FIG. 19/III

FIG. 20/III

FOREARM AND HINDARM DEFECTS IN SLEEVES C, D, E

Looking at the sleeve on the figure from the side, observe the fit of the forearm and of the hindarm (Back line fold) which should hang straight and taut, without creases, drags or unnecessary fullness (some folds will, of course, always appear when the arm is moved, particularly in loose sleeves). The following defects—three on the front and three on the back—must be mentioned:

C—FULLNESS DOWN THE HINDARM

The sleeve appears to be sagging on the hindarm, with **loose folds** coming down almost to elbow level (sketch-Fig. 19). There is no creasing *across* the sleeve.

The correction is quite obvious: **pulling up the hindarm** with the result that the **back part of the crown is hollowed out or flattened more** (Fig. 19). Undo the seam about 8 cm above and below point B before correcting. Point B, in

coming down lower, *shortens* the Back line and so pulls it up. Before pinning the seam tighter it must be *tested for comfort with the arm raised* (detail). The main 'pull' of a sleeve is normally felt along the Back line, continuing across the Back of the bodice.

Fullness down the forearm. Loose folds give the front part of the sleeve an untidy appearance. To correct, **take up the sleeve at and near point F,** after first undoing the armhole seam as described above. Pull up the forearm (0·5–1 cm) until it hangs straight (Fig. 20): this **hollows and flattens more the front part of the crown**.

The two defects—back and front—may appear together, which usually indicates that the whole sleeve head is *not sufficiently pulled up at B and F for the particular shape of the shoulder*.

When correcting one side only—back or front—care must be taken *not to upset the correct balance* of the sleeve (test on the stand).

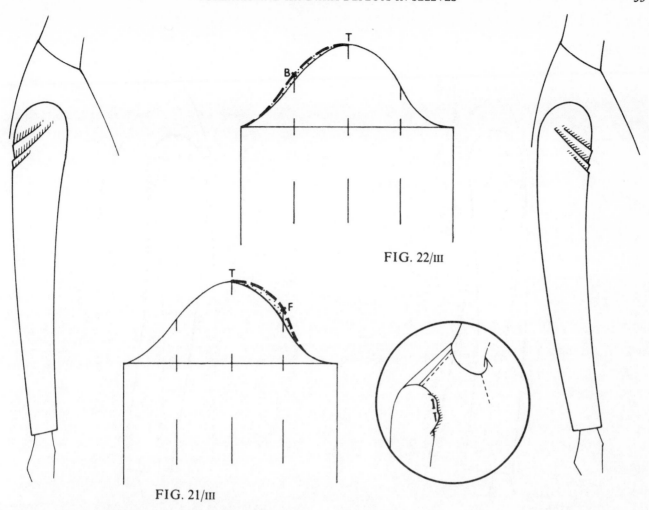

FIG. 22/III

FIG. 21/III

D—TIGHT DIAGONAL CREASE FROM FRONT TO BACK

This is a slanting tight 'drag' across the top of the sleeve. The crease usually shows clearly where the pull comes from—the front of the shoulder bone, which is obviously higher or more prominent than average (Fig. 21).

Letting out the crown above point F releases the tightness and provides more ease for shaping over the shoulder bone.

Tight diagonal crease from back to front. Here the pull is in the opposite direction, i.e. from the back where the sleeve feels tight, particularly when the arm is moved slightly forward. The defect may be due to an over-developed back shoulder, or simply to the sleeve having been pulled in too much at this point when it was set in.

Letting out the crown near point B (Fig. 22) releases the tightness, but this should be tested on the figure for the minimum amount required so as not to produce the opposite defect.

It will be easily understood that a sleeve set into an armhole may not only be too 'pulled up', i.e. tight at a certain point of the crown (as described above), but sometimes also 'too loose', giving **unwanted height on the crown edge** for a particular shape of shoulder and arm. Such unnecessary looseness at the crown edge (not to be confused with the necessary ease or fullness *along* its edge) is simply removed *by pinning the surplus height out* (detail).

Thus the outline of the crown may change as a result of direct fitting on the figure.

The above defects—diagonal creases or creases very similar to them—are sometimes an indication that **the sleeve is not balanced correctly** and either swings too much forward, so that with the arm *down* creases develop from the front shoulder bone, or is set in with a backward swing, causing a pull from the back when the arm moves even slightly forward. The hang of the sleeve should be *tested on the stand* and, if necessary, the sleeve re-set, as explained in the next section. If, however, the *hang* of the sleeve is found to be normal, correct as explained above, by letting out the crown.

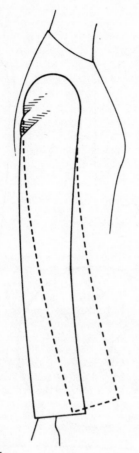

FIG. 23/III

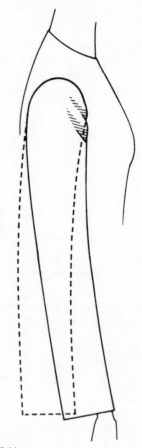

FIG. 24/III

E—FOLD AT THE TOP OF THE HINDARM

This fold looks like surplus material at the back of the sleeve (Fig. 23). It shows when the arm is held straight down and is **due to a forward pitched hang of the sleeve** (as Fig. 11-b). It can be **corrected only by re-setting the sleeve** to hang in a straighter line. One must decide whether this is desirable or not, as a forward swing, *if not* excessive, is suitable for many types of garment when forward arm movement is important. It is also suitable for some figures, e.g. very stooping figures with round shoulders may need it. Therefore in these cases, when above all a comfortable fit must be ensured, this fold in the *back* of the sleeve cannot be avoided.

Fold at the top of the forearm. The same defect in the front indicates that **the sleeve swings back** (as in Fig. 11-c) and **must be corrected** (Fig. 24). As already stated earlier, a swing to the back makes a sleeve uncomfortable in

wear and impedes arm movement. It may happen as the result of altering the Inset points at the fitting by pulling up point B too much. It is obvious that the sleeve must be turned in the armhole and **re-set to hang straight down.**

Both the above defects involve a slight **turning of the sleeve in the armhole**: in the first case moving point B of sleeve crown up and point F down, in the second—the other way round.

This covers the main defects encountered in sleeve fitting, defects which are due largely to difference in the shape of the figure (shoulder and Top arm) and also to posture. No special indications can be given for unusual or fancy sleeve styles and various fashion effects which must be dealt with according to circumstances.

In conclusion, it may be useful to go through **a list of possible sleeve troubles**, if only to see which of these can be easily eliminated by careful workmanship, attention to detail and understanding of the sleeve pattern.

A SLEEVE MAY FIT BADLY because:

(*a*) the bodice fits badly (wrong balance, shoulder slant, etc.)

(*b*) the armhole is badly shaped and fitted (e.g. too loose)

(*c*) the sleeve pattern is faulty (e.g. insufficient elbow spring)

(*d*) wrong type of sleeve is used (e.g. Two-piece for tight sleeve)

(*e*) sleeve is carelessly cut out (off the grain)

(*f*) sleeve is badly assembled (seams twisted, stretched)

(*g*) setting-in is incorrect (for current fashion, or type of garment)

(*h*) sleeve is set into wrong armhole (the right into left)

(*i*) crown edge and armhole are *not related in size* (not checked)

(*j*) **sleeve hangs badly**

(*k*) **shoulder and arm are not of average shape**

Only the last two points, connected with individual variation in the shape of the figure, belong to real sleeve fitting: everything else can be avoided by careful workmanship, and above all by understanding how the sleeve is constructed and how it is joined to the armhole.

Thus in spite of the apparently numerous possibilities of mistakes in sleeves, to which the constantly changing fashion may add its complications, with some experience, working skill and knowledge of the basic principles, few sleeve troubles need be expected, and this even when no individual fitting is possible. This is proved by the successful results obtained in most ready-to-wear garments produced by the wholesale manufacturing trade.

SPECIAL CASES OF SLEEVE ADJUSTMENT

Pattern adjustment

As was explained in Chapter III the highest point of the sleeve (point T) should come to the highest point of the shoulder, which is not always where the actual *shoulder seam* appears on the figure. Hence the difficulty of making a *firm rule* about matching the top of the sleeve to the shoulder seam or to some other *definite* point to the front or back of it. Though one can work this out *theoretically* by applying the sleeve pattern to the bodice armhole, it is still subject to possible change on the figure, since the armhole itself may be affected by various fitting corrections.

At a practical fitting this does not present a very serious problem since the sleeve crown may have to be reshaped in any case to suit the shape and posture of the figure: thus, for instance, a simple increase in the *depth* of the crown already changes the length and shape of its edge. Moreover, at a fitting, the correct matching of points is easier because one can see where the highest point of the shoulder actually is and so match the top of the sleeve to it. It is important, however, to understand this also theoretically, and to know how **a correct adjustment of crown to armhole** should be made in the pattern.

Thus, when dealing with a figure requiring **a longer than average back armhole** (e.g. for a very stooping figure) one must see to it that *the back crown edge* of the sleeve is long enough to match it, while allowing for some ease above point B and for a *forward placed* sleeve seam.

At a fitting this may sometimes entail letting out the sleeve on the back edge of its seam while losing the same amount on the front edge. In practice, however, this does not often arise because in such cases the back armhole usually needs to be *tightened by manipulation* near the shoulder blade and so finally matches the sleeve edge. When dealing with a pattern, however, the aim must be to get the crown edge a little longer, not only in the front part, but also in the back. Thus, *when the back armhole becomes longer*, whether for reasons of individual fit or as the result of a change in the basic bodice construction, the back crown edge must be increased, and the back 'half' of the sleeve will then become wider than the front: the sleeve is *no longer equally divided lengthwise* by its Top line.

There is more than one way of achieving such an adjustment in the pattern. One method has already been shown in the construction of a French Tight Fitting sleeve where the Top line is not in the middle: the seam is 'moved forward' by reducing its front edge and adding the width removed to the back edge, so that on the figure the seam is shifted to the front. This improves the fit of a tight sleeve which must mould the arm, but is not essential in a loose style. (See Dress Pattern Designing p. 69).

When the required increase in length of the back armhole is small, not exceeding 0·5–1 cm, the same effect can be achieved in a simpler way, **by moving forward the Top line** of the sleeve, as is done, for instance, in the Kimono construction. In such cases care must be taken that the new point T, drawn between 0·5 and 2 cm to the front of the middle line, is on the same level as the original one by slightly *raising* the front of the crown curve. Such a change need not affect the rest of the crown edge. Instead of displacing the whole Top line, a simple balance mark in this position can be used instead, with a slight raising of the front curve.

Therefore, to sum up, the back crown edge of a sleeve pattern should always have a little extra length compared with the corresponding part of the armhole and thus careful **measuring of sleeve and armhole** is always an **essential preliminary step** in all such adjustments.

FASHION ADJUSTMENTS

These vary with every definite fashion change affecting the setting in of the sleeves, i.e. with every change in the shoulder line silhouette.

At the moment it may be useful to note a trend towards a higher set of the sleeve on the shoulder, often with clearly visible fullness in the crown. In this connection, it must be remembered that not only has the sleeve crown itself to be raised (i.e. gain extra height as described in 'Dress Pattern Designing'—Chapter VIII), but the armhole also has to be placed higher, particularly in the front part of the shoulder. This is, naturally, bound to affect the sleeve head which may look different from the basic version.

NECKLINE AND COLLAR FITTING

The fitting of necklines must be considered as part of bodice fitting. Collars, however, with a few exceptions, are cut separately, and their fitting involves problems both of the set of the collar and of the way it is joined to the garment.

NECKLINES

The actual cut and fit of a bodice can often be affected by the shape of the neckline. Some fancy necklines may, for instance, require a different use of the surplus fullness of the bust dart. It is not, therefore, just a matter of correcting a neckline shape *when fitting*: the whole question of the neckline fit has to be considered at an earlier stage, i.e. when planning the pattern of the bodice.

Necklines appear in a big variety of styles, particularly if one includes the many draped styles. It is useful, however, to consider first **the three basic necklines** which can serve as models for a big number of more fancy ones, similar both in the way they are cut and in the way they are dealt with at the fitting. These 3 basic shapes are **the Round, the Square and the V-shaped necklines**.

Round necklines can in most cases have some fullness eased into them (apart from style fullness, such as visible gathers, smocking, etc.). Easing, or even gathering, does not spoil their shape—it only increases their curve. It is therefore usually possible to dispose of some of the bust dart fullness in a round neckline. This is important and is often taken advantage of when fitting a person with a very large, and particularly a very prominent bust, for

whom a deeper bust dart is generally suitable: *part* of such a deeper dart can be eased into a round neckline and the fullness made to come over *the middle* of the front where it is quite becoming.

Apart from these special cases, a round neckline is generally an easy neckline to fit on figures of all shapes and sizes, as it can always be pulled in tighter or released (widened) without losing its shape. The only difficulty which may arise is in the way it is to be finished off (by binding, facing, setting into a band or narrow yoke, etc.), and this must be borne in mind while fitting, as some methods of finish will make *easing* more difficult than others. In some cases, style and fabric permitting, small darts and tucks are used for the same purpose.

Exceptions to the above way of dealing with round necklines may be **styles where a tight, i.e. flat fit is essential**. An example of this is a very cut away neckline which must not be allowed to slip off the shoulders, yet cannot always be 'pulled up' and eased conveniently because this may curve its edge *more than the design permits*. Some wide boat-shaped necklines belong to such styles.

Here, on the contrary, the neck edge of the pattern must be tightened, either by cutting it smaller (to allow for stretching) or—more correctly—by **increasing the bust dart** (see Modelling Exercise XII, Chapter One). As shown by this modelling exercise, a deeper bust dart has the effect of *tightening the bodice over the chest* and so making the neckline tighter also. However, since in this case no excess fullness can be left in the neckline because

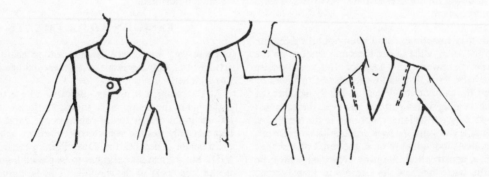

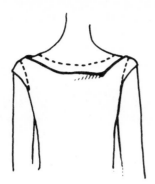

FIG. 1/ɪv

FIG. 2/ɪv

this would loosen it and spoil its shape, the increase must be added to the existing bust dart, more often an underarm dart, thereby making it deeper.

If, at the fitting, such a neckline, e.g. a wide boat-shaped style, is found to be too loose (Fig. 1), with a tendency to slip off the shoulders, then—*turnings permitting*—the looseness should be smoothed away in both directions, from the CF towards the armholes, and the neckline re-outlined *inside* the original line, i.e. higher on the shoulder (for more details see over the page 'Correcting a neckline').

Thus, from a fitting point of view, round necklines can be divided into those which can be tightened by easing and those which must be kept quite tight and flat.

One must remember, of course, that tightening across the chest by increasing the bust dart may tend to give a very flat and strained effect above the bust, and this is not always suitable for every figure. These are, however, details of style and individual becomingness, which can only be decided by the fitter.

The V-neckline is quite **unsuitable for easing** (unless it is of a semi-curved shape), and should be quite tight if gaping is to be avoided (Fig. 2). Easing makes a straight line curve, and a perfect V-neckline is impossible unless the two lines forming the angle are taut and straight. This can be ensured only by keeping the whole top part of the bodice below the neck *quite flat*, with **no ease in the basic neckline** (see end of Exercise VII, Chapter One). An average bodice with a *fairly deep* bust dart is expected to fit like this unless, for some reason, part of the Shoulder dart had intentionally been left in the neckline (or the figure has a very hollow chest).

The cross-over usually follows the same principle, i.e. if its edges are to be kept *straight and taut*, there must be no looseness in the CF part of the basic neckline: but this, of course, need not be the case if some curving is acceptable or, according to the style even desirable, e.g. to achieve a lower crossing point of the two lines.

The Square neckline is another style which tends to 'gape' very easily on the figure. To make it lie flat it is again essential to have *a flat fit of the basic neckline* before the square is outlined. With a very wide square it

may even be advisable to increase the bust dart, as mentioned above, in order *to tighten the fit across the chest*.

Various other shapes of neckline include very wide boat-shaped styles (already mentioned), 'straight-line' necklines running from shoulder to shoulder, or even dropping off the shoulders; various fancy styles such as 'heart-shaped', U-shaped, etc. Finally, the 'strapless top', with its very tight edge above the bust, must also be mentioned (sketches).

Some of these necklines *need tightening*, often quite considerably, as in the case of the 'strapless top' (usually a 50% dart increase); some just have to be kept *quite flat* in order to prevent gaping (heart-shaped or 'straight-line across' styles); while some *can be eased* in a curved part if any tightening is necessary.

With all this variety the point to stress is that adequate tightness for each style of neckline has to be considered at the pattern cutting stage. Only small adjustments should be left to the fitting which is mainly concerned with the checking of the actual shape, i.e. the depth and width of the neckline on the figure.

CORRECTING A NECKLINE AT THE FITTING

This is not particularly difficult provided turnings are available. After undoing the shoulder, a square or a V-shaped neckline which gapes is smoothed away from

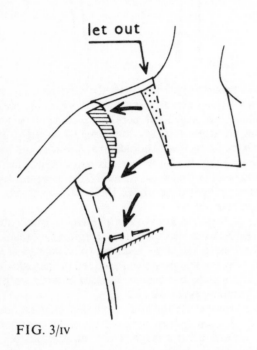

FIG. 3/IV

the neck (0·5–1 cm, sometimes more) until it appears to regain a reasonably flat fit on the figure: it is then re-outlined closer to the neck, making use of the turnings (Fig. 3).

It is therefore usual, and generally advisable, particularly in the case of a big neckline, **not to cut out a neckline before a fitting**, but only *to mark its shape*, so that its *tightness can first be tested on the figure*. If this is inconvenient, very good inlays should be left, mainly at the neck end of the shoulder.

The outer end of the shoulder which is smoothed away from the neck to flatten or tighten a neckline goes in some cases into the armhole, i.e. is simply *pushed out*, but a small amount only since *this loosens the armhole*; or it is added to the bust dart (as in Exercise XII, Chapter One). Thus, while correcting a neckline, **some surplus fullness** often has to be moved down the armhole to be added to an underarm dart. It must not be allowed to spoil the armhole by loosening it too much, though sometimes a slightly easier armhole is quite acceptable.

Raised (built-up) necklines. The main fitting problem here is connected with the amount of ease at the base of

the neck allowed in the pattern before the neckline is extended upwards. Referring to the construction of this pattern, it will be remembered that, in order to get enough width on *the front top edge* of a *close fitting* built-up neckline (particularly, for example, for a person with a forward sloping neck), it may be necessary to make the pattern looser *at the base of the neck*. Yet, as this looseness is not actually needed here, but is simply unavoidable, it must never be exaggerated: in fact if it is possible *to stretch the top edge* with an iron later, it is better to use a little less than the pattern appears to require by measurement. **N.B.** In the case of a raised neckline which stands away at the sides and so *must not fit close to the neck*, even less of this extra ease at the base of the neck—if any at all—is needed in the pattern.

At the fitting, a **slight loosening or tightening** of the top edge may be achieved by letting out or taking in the raised part of the shoulder seam (Fig. 4). This is not a difficult adjustment when the amount is small. In suitable fabrics most of the unnecessary 'looseness' at the base of the neck can usually be shrunk away, without affecting the width at the top edge. This is therefore a type of neckline which can be made to fit better partly by manipulation.

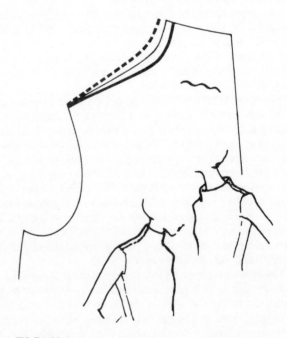

FIG. 4/IV

Draped necklines. These are of different shapes and a reasonably correct cut is essential. It is difficult to drape a neckline entirely on the figure at a fitting, and it should at least have been tested on the stand to make sure that the amount of fullness allowed for the number and depth of folds required is adequate.

The Cowl neckline, which is probably the most popular draped style, has a special fitting problem: the checking of its depth. Even if correct for the style, it may appear too high on a figure with a high bust, or too low on a flat-chested one.

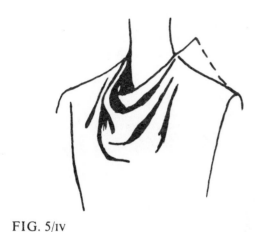

FIG. 5/IV

It is important to understand that a cowl neckline is made lower or higher not by cutting it out more or less on the top edge, but by *dropping it from NP's* to make the top fold longer and so deeper, or vice versa, by *taking it up at NP's* to make the top fold shorter and the neckline higher. If one attempts to *cut out* a cowl neckline, the top fold, which is always the deepest and the one that 'sets' best, is simply cut away and the cowl looses much of its draped effect. Unless this is specially required (and then the designer's idea must be carried out), the deepest fold is generally retained and the depth of the cowl is regulated from the Neck Points (Fig. 5).

There are other draped necklines based on the cowl, e.g. the heart-shaped style (as sketch). Here again the main problem is to have *sufficient length in the top fold* to enable it to be arranged as the design requires (e.g. held by clips): this also would be controlled from the NP's.

As to the question of whether a cowl should always be cut on the true bias, it must be stated that this is not essential, though on the whole much more usual. Actually, either bias or SG can be used down the CF line, but there is a difference in appearance which must be noted: bias folds are more 'set' and more precisely shaped; SG folds are more untidy, less clearly defined. Fashion has much to do with this: there are times when the SG down CF may be used quite deliberately to avoid the very 'set' appearance of bias folds.

Moreover, a true bias cowl, unless it is *a separate inset part*, means cutting the whole bodice front on the bias, and this, for one reason or another, may not always be desirable.

The draped fold, slightly raised at the neck, is a simple form of draped neckline to which the basic rule of *sufficient* ease at the front neck also applies. The tightness must be just right, not too tight for the shape of the neck (e.g. in the case of a forward sloping neck), nor so loose that it forms a small cowl instead of a *stretched* fold. Here again any adjustment would be from the Neck Points, i.e. by letting out or taking in at the neck end of the shoulder.

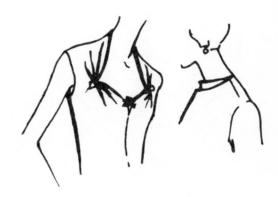

The neckline under an attached collar. Often this is the basic neckline or one slightly cut out; but of course it may be any shape. At certain periods in fashion most collars are set into necklines which are *slightly cut away* so that the collar cannot fit close to the neck; at other times collars are required to *cling* as much as possible to the neck and all necklines are then close fitting (See also Chapter Two—Points 2, 3 and 16).

COLLARS

To understand more clearly what is involved in collar fitting the following Modelling exercises will be found quite useful.

MODELLING EXERCISES

A—Modelling a Flat collar.

Take a piece of leno—a rectangle 30 × 25 cm—and place it with the longer edge (L–SG or selvedge way) to the CB of the stand, so that ⅓ of the length (10 cm) comes below the neckline. Pin at the neck, with a second pin 7·5 cm lower down the CB (Fig. 6). Starting from the CB, cut the leno following the neckline of the stand, but leaving a 1 cm turning. The scissors should be moved slightly upwards after each fairly short cut. Three or four cuts usually bring the line to just beyond the centre of the

shoulder. Apply the leno well to the stand below the base of the neck and bring it round to the CF, snipping the small turning where necessary (side, front), to make the collar lie quite flat (Fig. 7). Care must be taken not to cut into the **inner or Sewing-on edge of the collar**, which must be *clearly outlined round the base of the neck*, so that later the turning above it can be trimmed away. In the front fold the leno back and cut it along the CF line.

Measure and outline **the Outer (or lower) edge** making the collar 6 cm wide all round. This is a perfectly flat collar, in this case a round shape; but any other *flat* collar style would be cut in the same way. When removed from the stand and examined on the flat, it will be found to have *a very curved Sewing-on edge* which matches perfectly the neckline of the bodice pattern (Fig. 8). This will be the case whatever the style of the Outer edge. **N.B.** A bodice could be placed on the stand before modelling and, in general, collars are often modelled over garments to match the neckline perfectly.

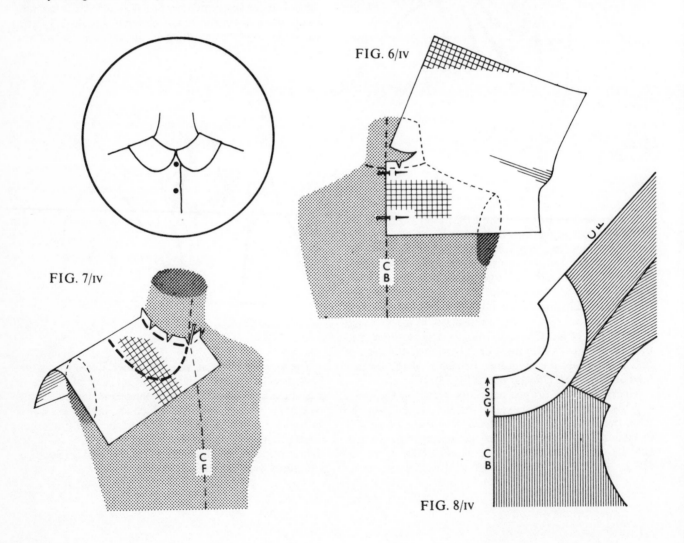

FIG. 6/IV

FIG. 7/IV

FIG. 8/IV

B—Modelling a Roll collar.

Using a piece of leno of the same size, model another flat collar, as above, but mark and cut out the inner edge *leaving no turning*. This can of course be just a copy of the first collar, as far as the neck edge is concerned, leaving however all the leno outside *uncut*.

Reversing the curved inner edge so that the main part of the leno now comes above the neckline, place it to the stand and pin at the nape, with a second pin a little above, as shown in Fig. 9; then—2·5 cm away from the CB—make a 0·5 cm cut into the curved edge (up to point Z) and *pulling it down to the neckline* pin point Z to the stand. 2·5 cm further make another cut into the edge, this time 1 + cm long: again pull the top end of the cut (point Z) down to the neckline and pin it carefully. A third cut, 2·5 cm further, can be 2 cm long. After pinning its top end (Z) to the neckline, *turn down the leno* to see and check the effect: it will be found that the CB edge will no longer come to the CB of the stand (Fig. 10), unless it is *pulled up to it*, as shown in Fig. 11, in which case, however, it will no longer lie flat but **form a small roll at the neck**.

Turn up the leno, as before, noting that it is now *closer to the neck* (Compare Fig. 12 with Fig. 9). Continue cutting into the curved edge of the flat collar at intervals of 2–2·5 cm making each cut just over 0·5 cm longer and each time pulling it down to the neckline of the stand, until the CF is reached (in this case 6 cuts from 0·5 to approx 4 cm long). Carefully draw the sewing-on edge, passing over the pins, and correcting it later to a good line. Then fold the leno down (Fig. 13) and it will be found that when the collar is pinned correctly *to the CB*, the roll will have increased.

N.B. To make the roll higher, the cuts must be made deeper, and this can be done either all round (as here) or only at a particular place, so that one can have, for instance, a collar which rolls in the back and a little at the sides, but lies quite flat in the front.

Outline the outer edge with the collar in its correct position, i.e. *turned down*, measuring 5–6 cm all round (or any other shape and width as required by the style); but this time the measuring is done *from the crease of the roll* (Fig. 13), so that only *the visible part* of the collar is measured: *the invisible part near the neck is the 'stand'*. Although the collar *appears* to have the same depth all round when on the figure, actually, when examined on the flat, it will be found to be *deeper where it rolls*. The stand of the collar thus forms quite naturally.

FIG. 9/IV

FIG. 12/IV

FIG. 10/IV

FIG. 11/IV

FIG. 13/IV

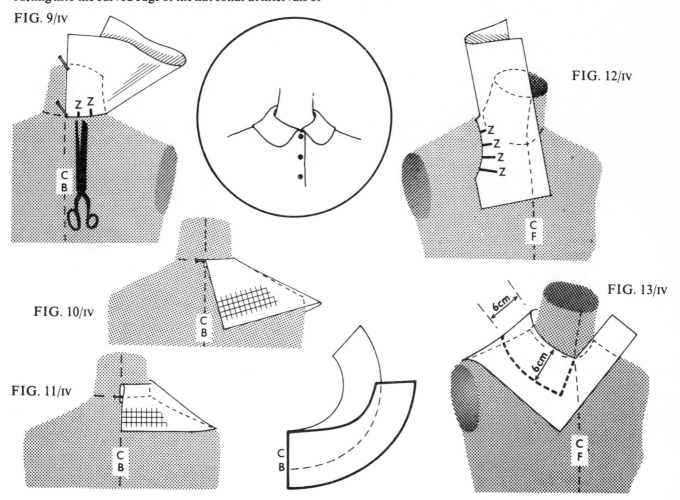

When the two modelled collars are superimposed and compared (detail), it becomes clear that **to achieve a roll in a flat collar** it is necessary to obtain **a straighter Sewing-on edge**, gradually moving away from the original deep curve, according to the roll required. It will also be observed that as well as having a less curved edge, the second collar has **a shorter Outer edge**, and that **extra depth** appears where the 'stand' of the collar is formed. All this information is very useful to a fitter.

One can, of course, go on experimenting in this way to obtain a big variety of shapes of collar, with different rolls—higher or lower—evenly distributed or with more roll in the back. The precise instructions and figures given here are merely intended to help in the *first* attempt (which otherwise is difficult to explain). Once understood, further experimenting should be quite free, guided only by the results obtained.

The main object of this exercise is to show what makes a collar set so that it rolls higher or lower at the neckline, clinging more or less to the neck. Understanding this makes it possible to prepare a collar for a fitting with more foresight and to know what to do with it at the fitting.

An increase or decrease in the roll of a collar is a frequent correction, not only because the style may have been wrongly interpreted, but also because the shape of the neck, as well as personal preference for a higher or flatter fit must be considered. The exercise shows how a collar must be *changed in shape to alter its set*; but of course the possibilities of correcting are always limited by the turnings available. Because of this, fitters— as will be explained later—often prefer to fit a collar first as a 'toile', on which they can make all the necessary corrections, before finally cutting the collar in material.

C—Modelling a Stand collar and a Turn-down collar. The Straight band and its fit.

Cut a strip of leno (calico) 6·5 cm wide (the width selvedge way) and 43–46 cm long. Pin the *middle* of the strip to the CB neckline of the stand and bring the two ends round to the CF, pinning them together along the SG (cutting away surplus length). Pin the lower edge of the band to the neckline of the stand at several places, including CF (Fig. 14). This is a simple **Straight Stand collar**, somewhat exaggerated in depth (the usual depth of a stand collar is between 2·5 and 5 cm).

It will be observed that this collar is quite loose *round the top edge*, particularly in the back where it stands away: it does not appear to fit the shape of the neck.

If, after unpinning the front ends, the straight band is *turned down* to form a 'stand' 2–2·5 cm high in the back, and running off to nothing on the CF, it becomes **a Turndown collar** much used in shirt blouses (sketch). In spite of its fairly close fit, it does not cling too well to the back and sides of the neck along its crease line.

If this collar is pinned to the basic neckline of a bodice with a wrap, previously modelled or placed on the stand (Fig. 15), and the neckline is opened on the CF and folded back to form **a rever neckline** (sketch), the collar will be found quite suitable for this style also: it is, in fact, a frequently used simple collar for open-necked shirts and folds back quite correctly.

Thus the same straight band, used differently, gives three different styles of collar. It is loose on the top edge as *a Stand collar*, not very close fitting on the crease line as *a Turn-down shirt collar*, and generally not very tight on the Outer edge as *a Rever collar*.

N.B. The collar in this case was modelled to its full length, i.e. *on both sides* of the neck, to show the set of the collar better.

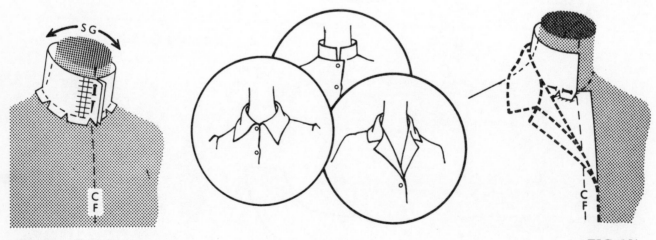

FIG. 14/IV   FIG. 15/IV

The Shaped band and its fit.

Take a strip 7·5 cm wide (L–SG) and approximately half the previous length. Pin one end (L–SG) to the CB *neck*, using a second pin higher, and leaving 0·5 cm below the neckline. Instead of taking it straight round to the CF, as before, *apply it well to the neck* (Fig. 16), snipping into the lower edge *up to the neckline of the stand*. Cut with a 0·5 cm turning, following the neckline, all the time smoothing the leno well to the neck of the stand, until the CF is reached (Fig. 17). The turning should be snipped where necessary, to keep the collar flat at the base. Cut away the excess length down the CF, which is not on the SG this time (Fig. 18).

It will be noted, while modelling, that as the top edge is applied to the neck for a tigher fit, the lower Sewing-on edge *curves up* above the X–SG level of the CB. If, after measuring and marking the top edge to the same height all round, the collar is removed and examined on the flat, it will be found to have become curved (detail) with the top edge a little tighter (shorter) than the lower Sewing-on edge, which of course always matches the neckline. This is a **collar moulded to the shape of the neck**. In a narrower width it can be used as **a shaped stand collar** (Chinese or Mandarin collar) which definitely *fits closer to the neck* than a straight band.

If this shaped band is turned down, as in the previous case, to form a high shirt collar, i.e. **a shaped turn-down collar**, it will be found to fit *very close to the neck* and even be unsuitable for some figures, e.g. for those with a short, thick neck. It does, however, cling better at the back and sides than a straight band, and has *a tighter fitting crease line*.

Used as **a shaped rever collar**, in an open front shirt, it is more suitable precisely because of this extra tightness which makes it set very neatly over the shoulders and round the back of the neck. Provided the stand it has formed is not excessive (2–2·5 cm) it is the best collar to use for blouses with *permanent* rever necklines, i.e. those always worn open in the front. It is also *the basis of the tailored jacket collar*, which can be said to be a development of it.

It must be noted that this collar must follow the exact shape of the neckline, and this can affect its Sewing-on edge. If the neckline is cut down lower in the CF (as it often is) the sewing-on edge must become less curved; otherwise there may be tightness in the join between the collar and the rever.

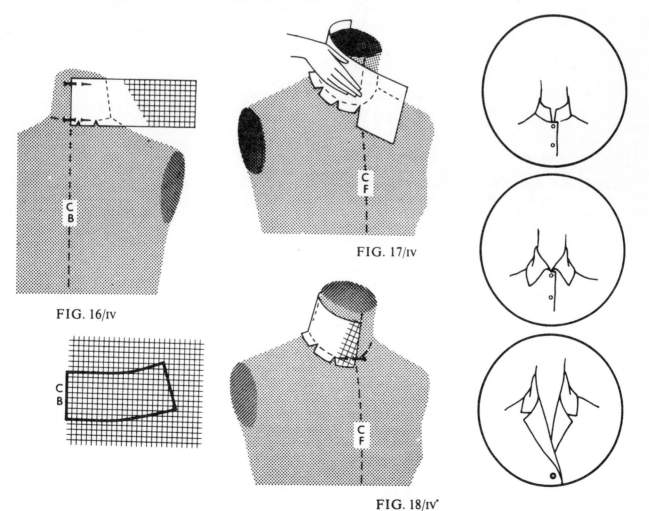

FIG. 16/IV

FIG. 17/IV

FIG. 18/IV

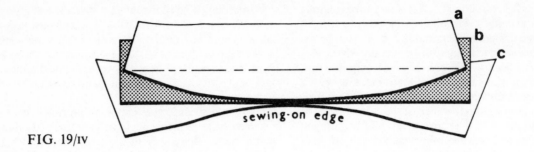

FIG. 19/IV

At this stage it may be useful to remember **the distinction between a 'tight' and a 'loose' collar**, especially in connection with styles which have either a *high*, buttoned up neckline (i.e. a tight neckline), or an open rever neckline (i.e. a loose neckline). The Turn-down collar with a convex curve on the Sewing-on edge is a 'tight' collar (Fig. 19 top collar), and is therefore mainly useful for a 'loose neckline', such as an open rever. Its crease line and outer edge are tighter, i.e. shorter than its sewing-on edge, and therefore for some styles it may be too tight, e.g. in a blouse which is to be worn *buttoned up at the neck*. The collar with the opposite curve on the sewing-on edge (Fig. 19, bottom collar) is a 'loose' collar and has both its crease and outer edge longer than the inner edge. It is often the most comfortable collar for the buttoned-up effect of a 'tight' neckline and may be too loose round its outer edge for a rever neckline (though much used for casual sports wear). The simple straight band (middle collar, Fig. 19) comes in between, and in spite of its somewhat untidy fit along the crease line, it is still a very popular type of collar.

Thus, in **summing up the modelling exercises** it will be seen that the defects one comes across in collar fitting are obviously very largely connected with the relationship between *the shape of the sewing-on edge* and the *length of the outer edge* of the collar.

The well known **defect** when **the neckline seam of a collar shows** from under its turned down outer edge invariably means an outer edge which is too tight (too short). If it is not possible or convenient to re-cut the collar with a longer outer edge (i.e. similar to collar 'c' instead of collar 'a'—Fig. 19), then—fabric permitting—*stretching the outer edge* with an iron may help to conceal the seam. This, in any case, is part of the manipulation technique in preparing a tailored collar, and the *principle* on which this is based applies to other turn-down collars as well.

It is easy to make a mistake in cutting a collar pattern, not only because of the difficulty in interpreting a collar style from a vague sketch, but also because it is not always clear which type of collar is suitable for or wanted by the person fitted (many people have their own definite idea on this subject). That is why it is a good plan, whenever in doubt, to make a preliminary 'test collar', i.e. a 'toile' in calico or mull which one can then try out for fit and effect.

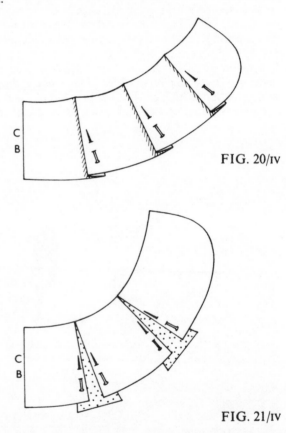

FIG. 20/IV

FIG. 21/IV

At the fitting of a roll collar (assuming a 'toile' is used) **if the collar is too flat**, it can be 'darted', i.e. small folds pinned out to **tighten the outer edge** (Fig. 20), thus *raising the roll*. **If the collar rolls too high** and clings too much to the neck, one or more slashes can be made in the pattern and wedge-shaped pieces set in to **lengthen the outer edge** and so *reduce the roll* (Fig. 21). Any extra depth required as the result of increasing the roll, can be added by pinning a piece to the edge. Cutting away, whether to reduce depth or simply to change the outline of the collar, presents, of course, no difficulty. In fact it is perfectly easy to *arrive at any shape* in this way, provided one is dealing with a test collar, from which a corrected pattern can then be made for cutting in material.

If an actual collar must be fitted, it can of course also be 'darted' by pinning the edge to raise the roll: a *new pattern* must then be made from it, incorporating this adjustment, after which—*turnings permitting*—the collar itself can be re-cut from the corrected pattern. Obviously only small alterations are possible in this case, as leaving too much turning in a collar may be very confusing at the fitting.

When fitting a turn-down collar, it can be tested and adjusted in the same way. Fig. 22 shows how darting (tightening) or slashing (loosening) a Straight band would affect the curve of the inner and the length of the outer edge of the collar in opposite directions, for two different effects.

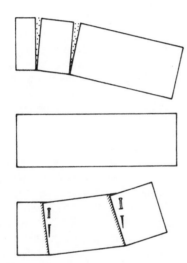

FIG. 22/IV

With **an open rever collar** it is also possible to tighten or loosen a little the fit of the outer edge by **adjusting it at the join** between the collar and the rever. Bringing the edges of the join closer together *tightens the fit*; letting out the seam, on the contrary, *loosens the fit*. The connection between the collar and rever (which is the folded over front neckline) must be clearly understood for, as already mentioned earlier, any adjustment of the neckline will affect the set of the collar.

Bias collars. These collars are not so easy to control from the point of view of fit because they are not usually cut to a definite pattern, but largely take their shape from the neckline into which they are set (it is of course possible to cut some bias collars from a pattern). They can, however, be made to alter their fit a little by manipulation.

To flatten the roll of a bias collar it is necessary to ease it into the neckline, as this changes its inner edge and, by *shortening it*, results in a *longer outer edge*. This of course

means that a folded true bias strip—the most usual shape of a bias collar—must be cut longer (at least 2·5 cm and up to 8–10 cm) than required by the neckline. The extra length, is eased into the neckline, sometimes all round, sometimes only at particular points (e.g. on the shoulders in a boat-shaped style). Thus, by shortening the inner edge, the outer edge, i.e. the *fold*, achieves *the extra length required for a flatter fit*. Occasionally, some stretching of the outer edge is also possible (see manipulation of collars below).

Rever collars cut in one with the bodice are also a little more difficult to control because of their connection with the fronts of the bodice. Such a collar can, however, be flattened or raised by re-shaping the back part in the same way as an ordinary collar; also by adjusting the length of its outer edge, taking it in or letting it out at the CB seam. As this usually has to be done on the actual collar (not on a 'toile'), the alterations are limited to what the turnings will allow.

MANIPULATION OF COLLARS

The fit of a collar is often improved by manipulation, and the Tailored collar is the best example of this. Basically it is only a slightly higher (tighter) collar than the shaped turn-down collar used with a rever in bodices and blouses. Its final effect, however, depends considerably on moulding it into the required shape by stretching its outer and, to a certain extent, its inner edges in order to make the crease line as tight and clinging to the neck as necessary. For easier manipulation a bias piece of canvas is generally used to interline the under collar over which, after pad-stitching, the top collar is then shaped.

The fit of a tailored collar therefore depends considerably on manipulation, and much that is learnt from handling it can be applied to dress collars as well. In the past, for instance, many simple round collars were cut a little short on the sewing-on edge in order to be stretched when sewn into the neckline: this made the crease line of the very slight *roll* come closer to the neck. Another example of manipulation is the easing and occasional outer edge stretching of the bias fold, already mentioned earlier.

In conclusion, it must be stated that it is most important to handle collars carefully, both when cutting out and assembling them. **The grain of the fabric** must be considered according to the style, as it certainly has an effect on the set of the collar. Usually the SG runs down the CB of a collar, but there are exceptions to this rule, e.g. simple narrow straight bands may be cut the other way, i.e. selvedge way. Bias collars, with a few exceptions, should be cut as bias *folds*, kept double and handled with the greatest care to avoid *twisting*, which is difficult to eliminate later.

Generally speaking, the design of a collar must always be studied carefully at the earliest stage not only from the point of view of the style to be interpreted by the pattern, but also from the point of view of its set and fit.

SKIRTS

In considering what constitutes the main problems of skirt fitting it soon becomes obvious that they are not only concerned with **the shape and posture of the figure**, but also with the **type of skirt fitted**. Quite apart from style and fashion, the 'line' (or silhouette) of a skirt matters considerably and may be found to be more, or less suitable for different types of figure. Thus, on a particular shape of figure the fitting of a Standard skirt will present no difficulties, while a Straight skirt will require some alterations, and a flared skirt may be quite unbecoming and so need many more adjustments or even complete re-shaping.

On the whole a well cut skirt requires little fitting— generally less than a bodice. However, it may happen that a *wrongly selected skirt line* (skirt block), or simply one which follows fashion too closely, will need a number of corrections simply because the line of the skirt does not suit the shape and posture of the figure. This naturally adds to the problems of fitting.

Broadly speaking, the average, fairly slim figure can wear any type of skirt and will need little fitting if the proportions are correct and there is no mistake in the construction of the pattern. But there is always the figure of not such good proportions which may, for example, look better in a straight or very slightly shaped skirt (the plump figure, thick through the middle), or, on the contrary, in a more shaped skirt (the tall, thin person). Their fitting difficulties will therefore be more individual, and be either simpler or more complicated according to which type of skirt happens to be in fashion. When fashion permits a choice of blocks (or when fashion is deliberately ignored), the right type can be chosen for each figure. But if, for one reason or another, the choice is restricted, additional fitting difficulties may arise.

It is therefore useful to begin by examining and **comparing the different skirt lines** (or silhouettes), and to note their effect on the different shapes of figure. The best way of getting a clearer idea of this is by **modelling the three basic skirts**: modelling shows how the three main types of skirt—**the straight, the standard** (slightly shaped) and **the fully shaped**—hang differently from the waist, and how in some cases this must affect their suitability for different figures, and so make fitting more, or less, difficult.

MODELLING EXERCISES

Using a length of tape or a strip of leno, mark on the stand the **waist line** (in its natural position), **the Hip line** 22 cm below the waist, but absolutely parallel to the ground (or to the lower edge of the stand), and **the Yoke line** 7 cm above the Hip line and parallel to it.

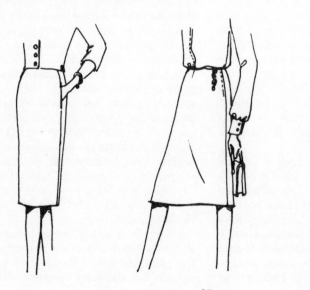

66

EXERCISE I—THE STRAIGHT SKIRT

Take a rectangle of leno 36 cm wide and 62 cm long. Leaving 2 cm above the waist, place the long edge (selvedge) to the CB and pin it at the waist, the hips and lower edge of the stand. Note or mark with coloured pencil the X–SG (crosswise straight grain) at hip level; then place the leno so that this pencilled line (X–SG) runs exactly along the hip line, i.e. quite horizontally (Fig. 1). Take it to the side and pin to the stand. Standing a little away, determine the position of the side seam first on the hip level (HP), and from this point fold back and crease the leno in a straight line up and down.

For the front, take another piece of leno of the same size and pin it exactly as the back at the CF waist, hips and lower edge of the stand. Again place the X–SG *along the Hip line*, and, at the side, fold and crease the leno for a straight (vertical) seam which can then be pinned to the back (Fig. 2). **The side seam** can follow the lengthwise SG, but will usually be made *to slope out a little to gain width at the hem* (Fig. 3). The sloping out, however, must be very slight—on an average 2·5–3 cm on every edge—as excessive sloping out of the side of a straight skirt can give an ugly hang to the seam. Nevertheless, a little widening is usual, as otherwise this perfectly straight, i.e. **tubular skirt** will appear to go in towards the hem on the figure and, *unless very short*, will be uncomfortable in wear.

N.B. Of course when the 'hobble' skirt silhouette is in fashion and the skirt *must* appear to go in towards the hem it is quite correct to use the perfectly straight pattern, without any sloping out of the side seams.

It will be seen that there is **much fullness round the waist** and this is characteristic of this type of skirt. This fullness cannot be avoided, i.e. it cannot be moved anywhere (e.g. down)—it **must be reduced at the waist**. In a simple straight skirt it is usually darted, four darts in the back and two in the front being the most popular arrangement, with the biggest amount taken out in the side seams (Fig. 3). But there are of course other ways of dealing with this fullness, such as gathers, draped folds, etc.

When, instead of just fitting neatly round the hips, the straight skirt is made quite wide, there is even more fullness in the waist: it then becomes simply *a full skirt*, gathered, or folded, or pleated, and the waist is dealt with accordingly. The main point to observe is that in all cases, whether the skirt is wide or narrow, the **X–SG runs in a horizontal line round the hips**.

Basically, therefore, the waist, hips and hem in a straight skirt are the same width and any sloping out must always be very small. There are of course other ways of increasing the hem width of the tight version of this skirt, such as wraps, slits, pleats, godets or other similar *inset sections*. The skirt can also be cut in gores, each of which

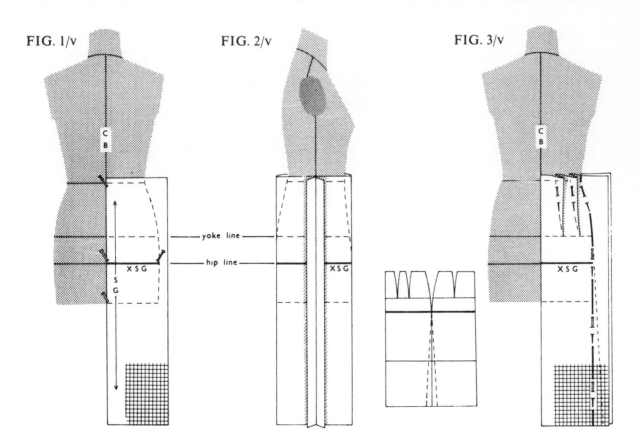

FIG. 1/v FIG. 2/v FIG. 3/v

can then be sloped out very slightly towards the hem, *without disturbing the correct horizontal set of the grain.* A straight skirt is thus most suitable for a fabric with horizontal stripes, for instance; and, in designing, much use is made of this, as well as of the considerable *and unavoidable* amount of fullness at the waist.

EXERCISE II—THE STANDARD OR SLIGHTLY SHAPED SKIRT

This type of skirt generally detaches itself more from the figure below the hips and stands away a little at the hem, so that it allows more freedom of movement than the tubular straight skirt. It follows the outline of a figure in motion. This *natural* widening towards the hem can be more or less pronounced, and there are several versions of this skirt, any one of which can be accepted as the standard skirt for a particular period in fashion. The point to note is that although the proportions vary slightly, the skirt is always wider at the hem and round the hips, and that **the side seams slope out naturally**.

Take a piece of leno a little wider than for the straight skirt (38 cm) and pin it as before to the CB, leaving a little more than 2·5 cm above the waist. Again *mark the X–SG on the hip level* (this may be done near the side seam only). Applying the leno to the stand, drop the pencilled line at

the side 1·5–2 cm *below the hip level*, and pin to the stand (Fig. 4). Note that the leno below the hip level now *tends to detach itself* from the figure.

For the side seam, fold back the leno in a straight (vertical) line and note that it will not follow the SG. Though straight when seen from the side, the seam will actually be 'off the grain' and will slope out a little (Fig. 5) when seen from the front or back, or on the flat. All this will have the effect of *reducing width at the waist* and increasing width towards the hem : some **fullness has in fact been transferred from waist to hem**.

Model the front in the same way, dropping exactly the same amount at the side (1·5–2 cm). Pin front to back, keeping the side seam vertical and allowing it to fall naturally, without following the SG (Fig. 6). Reduce the waist as in the previous skirt, but there will now be **less waist fullness to deal with** and so all the darts will be smaller.

Carefully mark the waist which, when the pattern is seen on the flat, will now be *slightly curved* (see pattern detail). The hip line and the hem will curve in the same way. In the straight skirt all these lines were quite straight, i.e. horizontal.

The hem must be levelled by measuring it up from the ground. **N.B.** This skirt can be made a little fuller by dropping the X–SG more than 2 cm below the hip level at the side.

FIG. 4/v   FIG. 5/v   FIG. 6/v

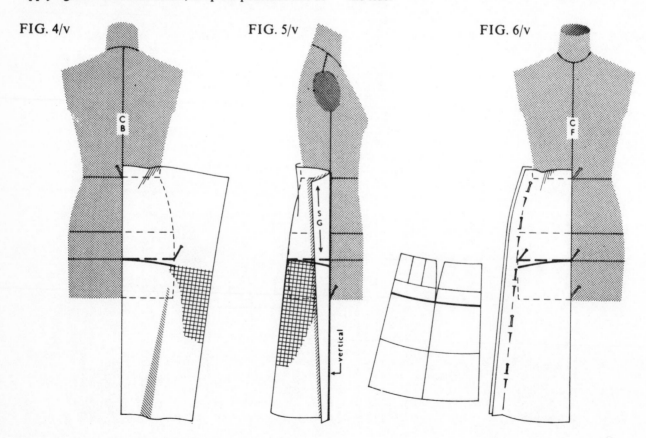

EXERCISE III—THE FULLY SHAPED SKIRT

Theoretically this skirt *has no fullness* at the waist as it is all transferred into the hem. It fits neatly from the waist to just above the hips and then flares out gently towards the hem. The side seam is completely 'off the grain'. The hem width is thus a 'natural' width which depends on the size of the waist: the smaller the waist (in proportion to the hips), the wider the hem.

Use a piece of leno 45 cm wide and 5 cm longer than the skirt length. For the back pin as usual to the CB, but this time leave 4–5 cm above the waist. Working from CB towards the side, apply the leno well to the stand in the upper part, i.e. above the hip level, snipping into the top edge to flatten it to *allow it to mould the* hips (Fig. 7). Snip as far as the waist but not beyond. The *X–SG will drop naturally*, until the waist is quite smooth and tight, and the fullness appears in the hem. After establishing the position of the side seam on a level a little above the hip line, fold the leno back as usual in a straight line (Fig. 8). The seam line must appear vertical from the side, though a slight swing to the back is sometimes acceptable.

The front is modelled in the same way, but as the figure here is usually flatter, the leno may 'drop' a little less and so give less width in the hem. Prepare the side seam in the same way, to join it to the back (Fig. 9). The top part of

the side seam, *when not attached to a bodice*, is usually shaped to the curve of the figure so that a *small 'dart' in the seam* forms here quite naturally. From the yoke level down, however (and usually all the way in dresses) the seam is quite straight, though sloping very definitely when seen from the back, front or on the flat. It is of course competely 'off the SG'. The pattern is very different from the straight skirt, i.e. much more 'shaped', and with all the basic lines (hip-yoke-waist-hem) more curved than in the standard skirt. The X–SG drops considerably below the hip level.

Although theoretically this skirt can have all its waist width 'moved into the hem', this is *seldom done in practice* for quite obvious **fitting reasons. Some width is usually retained in the waist** to allow for better shaping to the figure *above the Hip line* where the figure may vary (e.g. have a big hip bone, or prominent abdomen) and so will not necessarily follow the *shape of the stand*. Provision for this must also be made in a flat pattern (block pattern) to enable fitting adjustments to be made more easily.

In a pattern of a fully shaped skirt cut on the flat it is also usual to avoid having the front narrower and the back wider, *as it appears to happen in modelling* (and as it was used in the past, e.g. in the Edwardian skirt), and to keep the **width evenly distributed** round the figure.

N.B. The top of this skirt, down to yoke level, is of course identical with the shaped hip yoke modelled to extend the bodice in Modelling Exercise No. II (Chapter

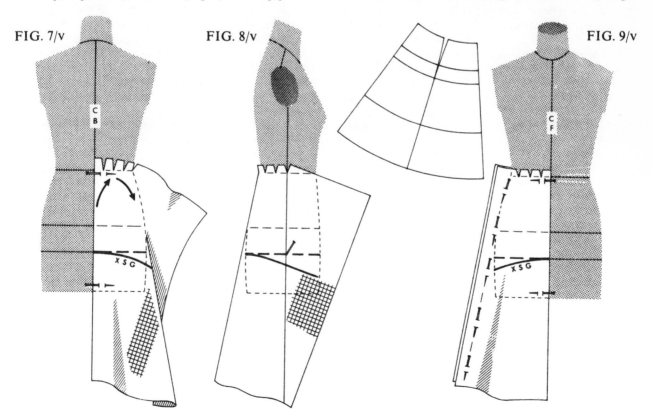

FIG. 7/v   FIG. 8/v   FIG. 9/v

One). The skirt is, in fact, an extension of such a yoke.

In **summing up the above modelling exercises**, it will be seen that a skirt gets a **different line or silhouette according to the way the grain of the fabric sets on the figure**, i.e. with the X–SG running horizontally round the hips, or dropping a little towards the side, or dipping considerably, until all (or most) waist fullness is eliminated from the top. **The 'surplus' fullness** can thus be moved (partly or entirely) to different positions, giving **more fullness (or ease) either above or below the hips**, as required by the style and the fashion silhouette. With the moving down of the surplus fullness, the skirt width *increases quite naturally* and it will be noted that **a 'shaped' skirt detaches itself from the figure** not only at the sides, but also **in the back and front**, in fact all round.

All these observations are useful from a fitting point of view. It is an advantage, for instance, when fitting if one can use a skirt line which is suitable for the figure, or at least avoid one which is *obviously unsuitable*. Some fitting troubles are due entirely to not appreciating this sufficiently.

It is also obvious from the exercises that the different skirt outlines will present different fitting problems. Thus the **straight skirt**, which is basically a 'tube', has quite a natural tendency to *cling too much to the figure* from the hips down and may thus be too tight on someone with overdeveloped thigh muscles. It may also *impede movement when worn long* (hobble skirt) or by a very tall figure, so that artificial hem widening will have to be considered (slits, insets, etc.). Getting rid of the *waist fullness may also be quite a problem* on a figure with large hips and small waist. The **shaped skirts** all have an easier fit below the hips as they are more detached from the figure and they have less or no fullness at the waist; but **the fully shaped skirt** often works out too *tight above the hips*, e.g. on a figure with prominent hip bones or abdomen, and its 'hang' and slight 'flaring' can be upset by a bad shape of figure or posture.

Nevertheless, it will be realized that it is not always possible to choose the most suitable skirt line in each case, for **the fashion line** will always predominate. When straight skirts are mainly worn, there is generally little use for the very shaped or flared skirt pattern, and vice versa. The choice of a suitable pattern, therefore, will, in the first instance, be decided by fashion in which *the length plays an important part*: though of course the pattern may be *adapted* a little (e.g. made straighter or more shaped) to suit the individual requirements of the figure.

A few words must be said about the **importance of the length of the skirt in relation to the different silhouettes**. Fashion determines the length of skirts and nothing changes so much in skirts as their hemline. From point of view of choice of a skirt it matters very much whether skirts are worn short or long.

Thus a straight skirt, for instance, even when quite tight, has few problems when it is worn short; but it can be most uncomfortable when long and is also often very unbecoming for a tall figure. The shaped, and particularly the fully shaped (slightly flared) skirt develops considerably more width round the hem when it is worn long and with just this difference in length it may present quite a different silhouette from its short version (the 'Maxi' and the 'Mini' skirts are a good example). The length therefore can have quite a decisive effect on the outline and *must always be taken into account* when fitting.

Finally, it is useful to mention again that the Modelling exercises point also to some problems of styling in connection with the use of certain fabrics. As already stated earlier, the straight skirt with the X–SG running horizontally round the figure is particularly suitable for fabrics with horizontal stripes, checks, or plaids, *when it is essential for the design* to retain the pattern of the fabric on a horizontal level (this of course may not be important in every case). With shaped skirts difficulties may arise when planning the pattern on some materials, or when making adjustments in seams at the fitting. Therefore, when dealing with a *special* fabric, the distinctive features of each skirt block must be borne in mind to avoid any complications later at the fitting.

MEASUREMENTS AND HOW THEY AFFECT SKIRT FITTING

On the whole measurements cause few difficulties in skirt fitting though some defects may be due to them. They can be taken differently—more tightly or more loosely: this depends entirely on the methods of work of the cutter and fitter. Where measurements are taken fairly loosely, obviously less (or even nothing) will be added for ease, and vice versa, so that it may be important to bear this in mind when fitting.

It is not easy to establish a precise **fitting allowance for a skirt**. Here again fashion is an important, in fact often a decisive influence, and at certain times all skirts are worn tighter, at other times looser. Often the style will dictate the tightness. Finally, some figures can wear tight skirts better than others, and personal taste also has to be considered. Methods of taking measurements may therefore have to be adapted slightly to different circumstances.

As already mentioned in the Course of Cutting* it is more practical to take measurements rather tightly: *nett measurements* are on the whole more reliable. However, since a larger figure takes up more room in a garment (e.g. in skirts when sitting down), larger figures should be measured a little more loosely and small figures more tightly *if the same allowance is used in both cases*. On the other hand, if all measurements are taken in exactly the same way, then the fitting allowance may have to be varied slightly according to the size of the figure. It can,

_____
* *Dress Pattern Designing*

of course, always be varied to suit a style or when considering becomingness (often intentionally giving a thin person more rather than less width for better effect). All this is of course entirely at the discretion of the cutter or fitter whose skill and experience must be freely exercised: no hard and fast rules can be laid down or much advice given on the subject.

The hip width allowance, i.e. the extra width allowed over and above the *tight hip measurement*, may be anything from 2·5–5 cm on the 18–20 cm level below the waist, and occasionally even less. It would be slightly more on a lower level, i.e. 23–25 cm below the waist. No more definite proportion than this can be given, and it is quite usual to have to alter a little the width of a skirt at the fitting for various reasons of style, fashion, wrongly taken measurements or simply personal preference. There is always a margin of possible error because of the numerous factors mentioned above. This is, however, a perfectly easy adjustment which seldom causes trouble, provided suitable turnings are available.

The waist allowance is yet another fluctuating quantity, particularly since *the waist measurement can so easily be taken too tight*. It should not be taken tighter than a skirt band (petersham) would be expected to fit. Although there may be some difficulty in obtaining a very precise measurement, the person fitted will always know what is acceptable to her, and it is more practical to be guided by this. Thus waist alterations are fairly frequent but again present little difficulty. Obviously in close fitting dresses and skirts the possibility of extra tightening always has to be considered but, for greater safety, this is better done directly on the figure.

The average figure has a definite **proportion between waist and hips**. Usually a difference of 26–28 cm between the two measurements represents a fairly straight, medium size figure. The larger (or the older) figure generally has less difference because of a bigger waist; while the figure with a small waist but large hips will have a greater difference between the two measurements. All this affects, of course, the fitting of a skirt.

There is nothing particularly difficult in **dealing with the waist fullness** when the difference is small, e.g. in most large figures. It is when the difference is big, i.e. on figures with a small waist in proportion to hips (often quite small sizes) that there may be more trouble, and extra means of disposing of the waist fullness have to be considered.

The dart arrangement, as planned in the pattern, may be wrong and need adjusting at a fitting. Thus, too many darts in the back, though correctly planned *by measurement*, may 'overshape' a figure, e.g. one with a 'sway back' (or prominent seat). In such a case it may be advisable to suppress more fullness in the front (in darts, gathers, soft draped folds) so as *to reduce the back darts*, thus enabling them to be shortened and flattened, to prevent them from 'poking'. The same consideration would

apply sometimes to the big dart concealed in the side seam: it may have to be reduced, i.e. let out, or increased, i.e. taken in for some figures according to the actual shape of their hip bone. The darts are an individual problem and cannot always be fixed correctly in advance by measurement.

SOME BASIC DEFECTS

The following are simple defects which seldom cause real difficulties in skirt fitting:

Skirt too tight: In a simple two-piece (back and front) style the width can be increased only by letting out the two side seams. The CB seam (where available) is also used for slight width adjustments.

In skirts with many gores it may sometimes be necessary to let out the other seams as well, either for reasons of style (e.g. to widen a panel) or in an emergency (because of insufficient side seam turnings). Considering the amount of work this entails, it would naturally be avoided as much as possible.

One can also achieve a *widening of a skirt by raising it from the waist*, i.e. moving the waistline down 1 cm or more and then lengthening the skirt at the hem. Sometimes this helps considerably when no more width is available in the seams.

Skirt too loose. Here the adjustment would be the reverse of the above. Again mainly the side seams are used to tighten the skirt, though sometimes the CB may be preferred (e.g. to achieve for it a 'slope' when it appears too straight); or a Panel may be reduced in width, both for style effect (more becoming) and for a tighter fit.

The skirt may also be dropped from the waist, i.e. the waistline marked 1–2 cm higher (provided there is enough turning) when a general *overall tightening* is desirable. The hem would be adjusted accordingly.

N.B. In a case of slight tightening or loosening, most fitters would also consider the machining of the seams just *inside* or *outside* the fitting lines as being a simple but effective way of adjusting the size.

Skirt too long. Shortening is generally done by turning up the hem more. In some cases, however, when the skirt is also on the tight side, it may be shortened from the waist to achieve the combined correction of shortening and widening. A pleated skirt may also be easier to shorten from the top (or from a hip yoke) if one wants to avoid altering the hem.

Skirt too short. Lengthening a skirt is usually done by dropping the hem which, when its full depth is used up, may require a facing. When some all-round tightening is acceptable as well, it may be possible to lengthen a skirt by dropping it from the top (possibly adding a waistband or small yoke). However, if, after dropping it from the waist, it does become too tight, letting out of side seams becomes necessary.

N.B. A tight skirt will generally be shorter on the figure than an easy fitting one. Therefore, to lengthen a skirt slightly, it is often sufficient to make it a little looser.

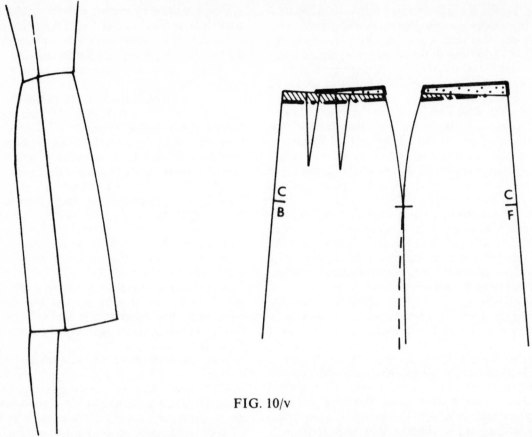

FIG. 10/v

Levelling the hem. Before any adjustment is made to the hem, it is essential to **make sure that the skirt hangs correctly** for often an uneven hem is due partly or entirely to the skirt fitting badly in the upper part (see lower). Thus a skirt may be pulled up in the back or front because of the posture of the figure; or on one side, because of uneven hips.

All this requires **correcting from the waist before the hem is dealt with**. Once the correct hang has been achieved, any further unevenness can be adjusted by letting down or taking up the hem itself.

SHAPE OF FIGURE AND POSTURE DEFECTS

Defects due to the posture and shape of the figure represent the main problems in skirt fitting. There are many cases in which the posture of the person fitted is responsible for various fitting troubles so that, in general, it can be said that a skirt hangs from the waist *as the person stands*.

THE HANG OF THE SIDE SEAM

The side seam is usually the first indicator that the hang of the skirt is not quite correct, for with an average posture the seam should be straight, i.e. as near to the vertical as possible (slight sloping in or out may be ignored since the figure is seldom completely motionless). If the **side seam does not hang straight**, the figure has not an average posture and either stands too much on the heels, i.e. leaning back, or too much forward. The hang of the skirt will be affected not only in the way the side seam falls, but in other ways as well. One can distinguish several cases which are clearly the result of *wrong posture*, though *the shape* of the figure may play its part as well.

Figure stands leaning back so that the **side seam swings forward** and the front hem pulls up and stands away from the figure (sketch and Fig. 10).

To rectify this defect the front of the skirt is dropped from the waist until it hangs straight. Extra height is thus built up above the CF waist, the new waistline running off to nothing, preferably beyond the side seam. Usually this is sufficient to correct also the line of the side seam; but if it still swings noticeably forward, then *the seam itself* must be altered in the lower part by taking off the back, and adding to the front. This of course would also be done when it is obvious that nothing else but the line of the side seam is wrong, i.e. the skirt itself *hangs* quite correctly.

A figure with a prominent abdomen usually has a similar posture and shows this defect (though of course not all

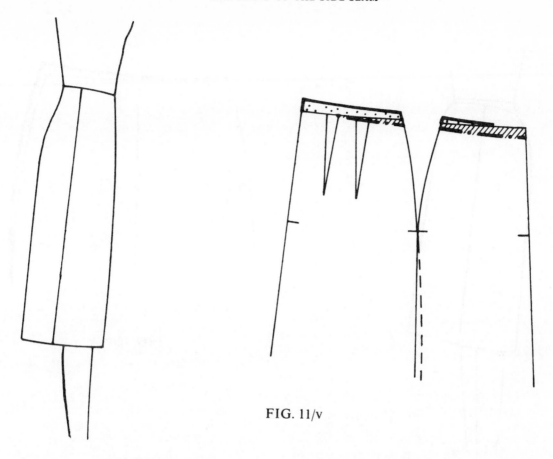

FIG. 11/v

figures leaning back are necessarily like that—many are quite flat). The adjustment would be the same but, in addition, it would probably be necessary also to *let out* the front seam in the upper part and possibly to have some slight easing of the front waistline, above the abdomen (see Fig. 13).

Where there is not enough turning to drop the front sufficiently, the back may be raised instead, i.e. the back waist hollowed out (dot-dash line Fig. 10) to gain the extra height required for the front. The two methods are often combined, half and half.

Figure stands leaning forward, so that the **side seam swings back**, and the back hem tends to pull up and stand away (sketch and Fig. 11).

The correction is the opposite of the one described above, and consists in either building up the back waist, which now becomes higher than the front, or hollowing out the front waist to pull up the front instead (Fig. 11). If the defect appears only in the side seam, with the hang of the skirt being otherwise perfectly satisfactory, then the seam itself must be replanned in the lower part, as described above, but in the opposite direction.

In connection with this defect it must be mentioned again that fashion influences the way women stand, as well as the position of the waistline, and even the way the waist in skirts is finished off (e.g. soft band, petersham narrow or 'raised', etc.). In the past an addition of height was made above the CB for most figures—small and large—partly to allow for the then popular slightly raised effect of back waist. At present this appears unnecessary, at least for the smaller figure, and the waist can be drafted on the same level, and is often even *lowered* in the back (for hollow waists). Extra height in the back however, may still be necessary for some figures because of their shape and posture, and for many larger figures.

A figure with a prominent seat will often have a similar forward posture and basically the same adjustment would be required. However, a warning must be given in this case: when dropped from the waist, the *back may tend to go in* below the hips (particularly in straight skirts) and this must be carefully *tested on the figure*. In such cases it is often a better plan to correct the back by making it a little more 'shaped', to detach it from the figure, as described lower (see Fig. 17); the side seam is then adjusted separately.

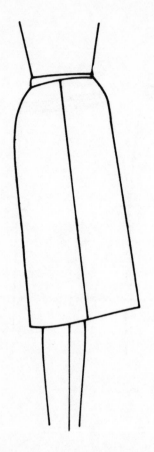

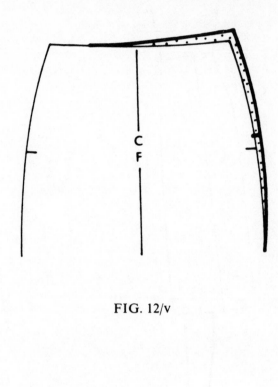

FIG. 12/v

Figure with uneven hips. Most figures are slightly uneven and also often stand putting more weight on one
leg. In most cases this can be ignored, unless it affects
the hang of the skirt considerably, so that one side is
noticeably pulled up, swings away from the figure and
the skirt never seems to hang straight (sketch and Fig. 12).

The correction consists in dropping the skirt from the
waist *on one side only*—the side which is pulled up by
the bigger hip, until it hangs quite straight. This means
building up the waistline only on one side. Since the
higher hip is also more prominent, the top of the side
seam usually has to be let out a little to accommodate the
bigger curve.

The side seam, may not only swing away from the
vertical line, but sometimes it may not run in a true
straight line, especially in the upper part when, for instance, a prominent abdomen may make it 'bulge' forward. Adjustment is best made on the figure, letting out
or taking in the seam *as necessary to straighten out the
line.* Since this is mainly caused by the figure being larger
in this particular part, it generally means *letting out* to
gain more ease, as well as to correct the line. The sym-
metrical outline of the side seam 'dart' is, of course,
affected and becomes uneven (Fig. 13).

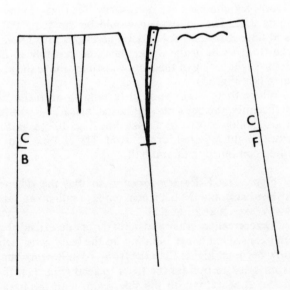

FIG. 13/v

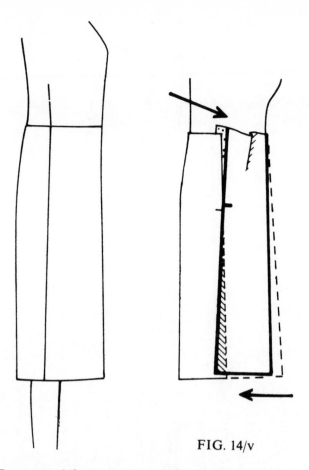

FIG. 14/v

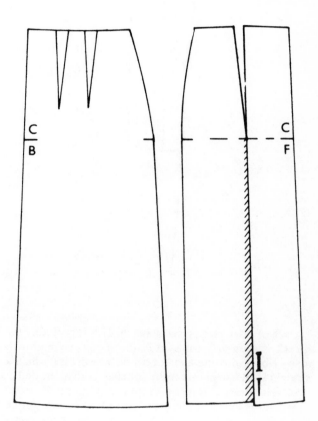

FIG. 15/v

Two more defects must be mentioned which are connected with both the posture and shape of figure.

Front of skirt falling away at hem. This happens mainly to larger figures with a prominent bust but very flat at and below the waist. In these cases the hips are usually small in proportion to the bust, i.e. the same measurement or even smaller. The defect shows more clearly in dress skirts, when attached to a bodice or cut in one with it. The hang of the skirt, though not necessarily of the side seam, is wrong; there appears to be too much width in the front and possibly not quite enough in the back (Sketch and Fig. 14).

The correction consists in **pulling in the front** to make it cling more to the figure, while the back is dealt with according to the posture of the figure.

At the fitting, undo the side seam and move the front edge up along the back (1·5–2 cm), while at the same time *reducing the width at the hem.* Dropping the front from the waist (i.e. building up CF waist) also helps to achieve a straighter or even slightly inward-sloping hang for the front, more clinging at the knees and tighter at the hem (Fig. 14). The back may be left as it is, and just widened a little at the hem; or, in the case of a *straight skirt,* it may have to be made a little more 'shaped', i.e. swinging out,

both to add some width on the hips and *to detach* it more from the figure: this is achieved by smoothing it *down* slightly towards the sides, exactly as when modelling a shaped skirt (Fig. 4).

Fig. 15 shows the *adjustment made on the pattern,* reducing the width at the hem in the front, which thus becomes straighter. The back may remain as it is or have a slight width addition in the seam, at the hem. It can also be dealt with as explained on p. 76 (third paragraph down), i.e. made more 'shaped'.

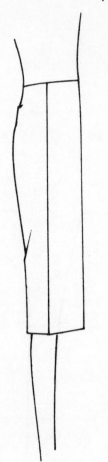

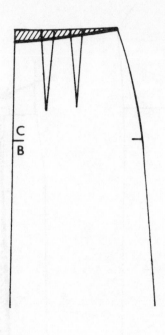

FIG. 16/v

Back of skirt sagging and going in. This is probably the most common defect in skirt fitting and is due mainly to a sway-back posture and hollow back waist for which a **straight skirt back is not really suitable**. Unlike the defect described above it is met with quite a lot in small sizes.

When the defect is slight, the correction is very simple and consists in pulling the skirt up at the back waist (Fig. 16) which is thus *hollowed out more at the CB*. The defect appears mainly in straight or slightly shaped skirts, and when these are fashionable many cutters believe in lowering the CB waist on all their skirt patterns.

When the defect is more pronounced, and on a figure with a prominent seat (particularly on a larger figure), it may be advisable to make the pattern of **the back more 'shaped' than the front** (Fig. 17), as could also be done for the previous defect. Pin out a dart at the waist, sufficiently big to give, in the slash below, 1·5–2 cm (seldom more) *extra width for the hem*.

Levelling of the hem. It will now be clear why the hem should never be levelled, i.e. taken up or let down, until after the skirt has been made to hang correctly from the waist, without pulling up at either front, back or side.

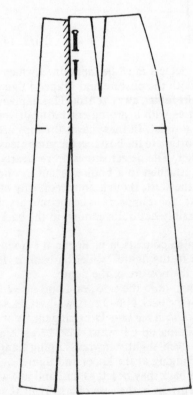

FIG. 17/v

SPECIAL DEFECTS CONNECTED WITH DIFFERENT TYPES OF SKIRT

Defects of Straight skirts. The fitting of these skirts has already been discussed in connection with Modelling and several defects **due to the line of the skirt**, and not the figure, have been mentioned, such as too much clinging to the figure below the hips, or tight hem restricting movement, or sagging in the back, or excessive waist fullness. One more defect which occurs frequently must be mentioned: **horizontal creases forming across the front** of a tight skirt at and below the hips when moving and particularly when sitting. It is due entirely to the skirt being a tubular shape, with no width expanding naturally. For the same reason a tight straight skirt tends to 'ride up' and to appear so short when sitting.

In most cases this creasing is simply ignored or accepted as an unavoidable 'fashion' defect. **Letting out the side seams** and sloping them out more towards the hem (possibly with a slight pulling up of the CF waist) helps to counteract this tendency to crease or at least improves the situation a little. The alternative is to increase the width right through, gaining more fullness at the waist as well, which may, however, change the line of the skirt too much.

Defects of shaped skirts. Although these skirts avoid most of the troubles of Straight skirts, they have their own difficulties. **The Fully Shaped skirt** and sometimes also the tightest of the circular patterns, i.e. **the Quarter circle skirt** which is similar in fit, can be too tight *above the hip level* and require letting out to fit the curves of the figure. This is of course due to the fact that the figure does not decrease from hips to waist *in a straight line*, but has curves such as prominent hip bones or abdomen, while the pattern is conical in shape and does not allow for such individual 'irregularities'. As a precaution, therefore, a pattern of such a **skirt is generally made wider in the waist than necessary** (5–10 cm more), to allow *for individual adjustment* on the figure. Sometimes, for the same reason, the width of the whole pattern can be increased to just over 1 cm down CB and CF (Fig. 18).

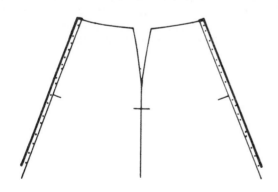

FIG. 18/v

At the fitting, if too tight, the side seam (sometimes other seams) can be let out, mainly between hips and waist. In the case of insufficient turnings, or for a general easing of fit *the whole skirt can be pulled up* from the waist (i.e. the waistline dropped) as explained earlier.

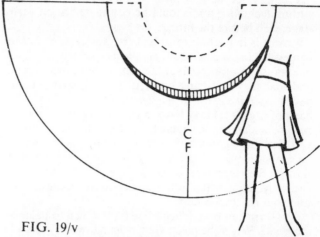

FIG. 19/v

Defects in flared skirts. The way the flares fall depends entirely on the hang from the top, i.e. from the waist or other line, e.g. a hip yoke edge. On some figures with a bad posture flares may be quite difficult to manage. Thus on a figure which leans back too much, **flares may tend to roll to the sides,** leaving the front quite flat—an ugly effect for an all-round flared skirt. **To correct** pull up the CF waist (or yoke edge, or other line) i.e. hollow out more the *line from which the flares fall* (Fig. 19). This will bring the flares back towards the CF and distribute them more evenly.

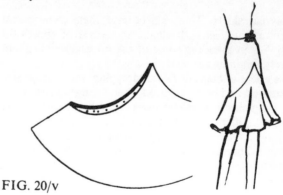

FIG. 20/v

The opposite correction would be required when the flares are 'bunched' at any particular point: the flares must be *pulled down* to make the top line flatter, i.e. less curved (Fig. 20).

There can, of course, be other defects in flared skirts, but most of these would be due to a wrong pattern, a bad lay on the material (wrong grain), sometimes bad design and occasionally difficulties with the texture of the fabric.

Defects in pleated skirts. It is impossible to consider all the defects which may appear in pleats, but most of them are due to *wrong cutting* (see Pattern Cutting course), careless assembling and general bad handling (e.g. stretching when pressing), rather than to the shape of the figure. Correct hang of pleats is very much part of the cutting technique and should be considered at an early stage, well before the fitting.

What it is important to stress here, however, is that to hang well, i.e. *in a vertical line*, pleats (particularly long ones must be supported) at the top, on both their edges, and that they will hang better if they fall over a comparatively *flat surface of the figure*. This means that the hang of the pleats may have to be *adjusted sometimes to posture or shape* of the figure (e.g. one with uneven hips); and also that figures with very prominent curves (waist, hips, abdomen) will not look so well in a *loose* pleated skirt as the slimmer and flatter type. Pleats, therefore, naturally hang better on, and are more becoming to some figures than others.

The waist can be a difficult line from which to balance the pleats. When the pleats start from a lower level, such as a yoke, which more often than not has a horizontal lower edge, the most difficult part of the figure is avoided and the pleats have a better chance of hanging straight.

There are various devices for helping pleats to hang better besides using a hip yoke: pleats can be stitched down part of their length, stitched across, caught together inside, etc. All this refers mainly to all-round pleated skirts: single pleats or groups of pleats have few difficulties provided they are cut correctly and handled with care.

Bias cut skirts. These skirts have their own special difficulties but, as with pleats, the secret of successful fitting lies in avoiding some of the mistakes right from the very beginning.

The effect of bias cut fabric 'dropping' must be clearly understood and borne in mind when fitting: as the fabric 'drops' it **gains in length but loses in width** so that the skirt becomes tighter round the hips and, *according to the hem width available*, develops larger or smaller flutes or flares at the hemline. All this must be allowed for when planning the pattern.

The weight and texture of the fabric have considerable influence on the final fit and line of a bias skirt, and with a looser woven, and particularly heavier material, the effect of 'dropping' will be more pronounced, giving the skirt a *closer fit*. Since long skirts have more weight, this effect is generally more obvious in long dresses: flares hardly develop in short bias skirts.

The width of bias skirts. It is difficult to give a definite rule for all bias skirts, for some are worn very short and tight. In general, however, it is safer to cut them with some extra width round the hips and lower, e.g. on a slightly widened Standard block. This can always be reduced at the fitting for specially clinging styles and on *suitable figures* (not all can wear bias cut skirts easily).

The hem width depends on the amount of flare required. Where no flares are wanted, particularly in very short skirts, less width can be used (1·25–1·40 m). For more pronounced flaring more width—often a considerable amount—is allowed, e.g. in long skirts. Thus the length is often the deciding factor.

The fit of a bias skirt changes as the material continues to drop, so before judging the fit, the skirt must be allowed to hang to gain in length. A first fitting does not always show clearly what **the final tightness** and clinging to the figure will be. It may continue to change—improve or otherwise—even during the early stages of wear. The hem may become uneven *if levelled too* early.

The main defects of bias skirts are generally connected with lack of hem width and overfitting.

Hem in the front rides up and appears short, mainly when moving and sitting. Forward movement of the legs stretches the fabric horizontally and so *shortens* it vertically. A looser fit can prevent or at least diminish this defect. It is also useful to allow *extra (2·5 cm) front length*.

Side seams puckering: This again is due to tightness, as the horizontal stretching reduces the length of the skirt while the *stitched seams remain the same length* and so pucker.

Uneven hem: This may be caused by the hem being levelled too early; or the skirt simply *continues* to drop, and so the hem must be done again.

This completes the survey of the most usual skirt defects and it is obvious that when skirts are cut correctly the fitting problems are seldom difficult.

THE FITTING OF TROUSERS OR SLACKS

In the fitting of trousers or slacks, problems of style and fashion are now involved as well as problems of actual fit to the shape of the figure. Since they are used as much for high fashion wear (e.g. evening styles) as for casual wear or for sport, the basic pattern has to be adapted to many more requirements. Close fitting right through, or just at the top, easy fitting or quite full—all these *style lines*, as well as the established adjustments necessary for various sports activities (such as riding, skiing, etc.) have to be provided for in trouser pattern designing.

It is therefore important to know the purpose for which the basic pattern of slacks will be used and to adjust it accordingly. Some of the adjustments will be just *fashion details*, such as extra tight or loose leg fit, a lowered (hipster style) waistline, etc.; but some will deal mainly with *the basic fit* of the pattern to make it suitable for the *shape of the figure*. It is with these that this chapter is concerned, since strictly speaking only this constitutes fitting.

Basically, all provision for changing the fit of slacks to suit an individual figure is already incorporated in the structure of the foundation pattern which can easily be adjusted to change (*a*) depth of crutch, (*b*) seat angle, (*c*) basic width across and (*d*) total crutch length. It is on the correctness of these *proportions* that the good fit of slacks mainly depends. Thus, in addition to the principal measurements—hips, waist and bodyrise—these proportions are needed in order to ensure that the top part of the slacks conforms as nearly as possible to *the shape* as well as *size* of the figure.

There are of course other measurements which are usually taken for the construction of a basic trouser pattern, such as the width of the knee, the calf and the ankle, which are used mainly for close fitting slacks; and of course the length, though the latter—easily adjustable to height of figure and style—does not affect so much the fit of the main part of the slacks. There are **two additional measurements**, however, which can be of great value in *controlling the fit* of the slacks *on an individual figure*: (*a*) the **high hip line**, taken 10–12 cm below the waist, i.e. a little above the Yoke line level of the skirt, and (*b*) the **total crutch length**, taken between the legs, from CB to CF waist. Both these measurements, though not essential for the construction of the pattern, are very useful when applied *to check its fit* on a particular figure.

The following are the most usual defects encountered in fitting slacks:

CRUTCH DEPTH DEFECTS

Both **excess and lack of crutch depth** are quite easy to establish on the figure. It may even be done with a pinned-up half-pattern. The top part of the trousers may either be not quite deep enough to reach to the waist comfortably; or it may be too deep and so appear loose between the legs. Both defects can easily be corrected at a fitting, either by raising or lowering the waistline, i.e. by dropping the garment a little from the waist, if too tight, and by pulling it up to fit closer to the figure, if too loose.

It must be noted that with a carefully taken Bodyrise measurement the mistake is not likely to be considerable, except perhaps on a large but *short* figure, when an additional check by 'total crutch length' measurement is advisable (see 'total crutch length' lower). It must also be remembered that there are other reasons for crutch tightness, which cannot always be attributed entirely to wrong crutch depth, as will be explained later.

SEAT ANGLE DEFECTS: BACK SEAM TOO SHORT OR TOO LONG

The seat angle (Fig. 21) is an important detail in the construction of the pattern, but it must and does vary,

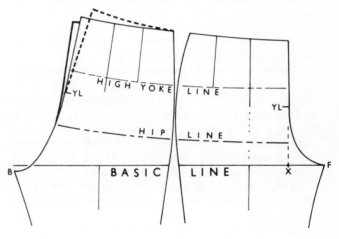

FIG. 21/v

not only for different purposes for which the slacks are used, but also for different shapes of figures. It is therefore one of the more usual adjustments made at the fitting.

The seat angle is increased, i.e. made more sloping (dotted line) when the pattern is used, for instance, for riding breeches (sitting posture) or for any activity where much moving and particularly bending is essential (though for some of these, slacks with a deeper or looser crutch are preferred). It may also have to be increased a little for figures with a prominent seat, a hollow waist or very stooping posture (curved spine).

The seat angle is decreased (thick line) or straight-

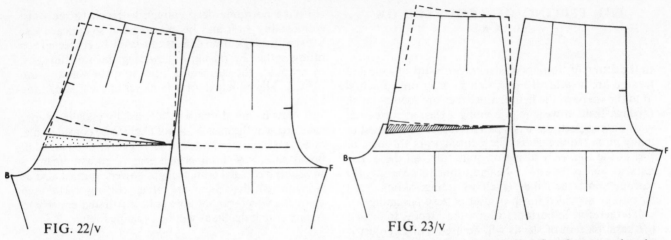

FIG. 22/v   FIG. 23/v

ened when the fit of the slacks must be very neat and flat in the back, without any baggy fullness. This happens of course in 'fashion wear' and is always possible on figures which are very flat and straight in the back, and generally slim round the hips.

In the pattern, to **increase the back seam length**, a horizontal slash is made at or just below hip level (Fig. 22) as far as the side seam (or sometimes only 2/3 out). When the slash is opened 1–2 cm, the CB seam is both *lengthened* and *sloped more*. The side seam 'dart' becomes smaller, i.e. closes partly, since the waist width, because of the sloping of CB, is reduced (less WR).

The opposite is done **to decrease the back seam length**, i.e. a horizontal 'dart' up to 2 cm deep, is pinned out on the same level (Fig. 23), which straightens the CB seam and shortens it *correctly* (i.e. not from the top), while at the same time increasing the waist width by making the Side seam dart become deeper. Some of this extra width may be transferred either into a second back waist dart, or preferably, into a front dart or pleat (fold).

At the fitting, if it is considered necessary to make the correction, the CB seam is opened and either *sloped more*, taking out some waist width at the top and then *raising the seam a little*, or, on the contrary, *straightened* by letting out at the waist, and then shortening the seam, as required, while the extra waist width released will have to be suppressed elsewhere. It must be clearly understood, that simply adding height or taking it off at the CB waist does not have the same effect without the sloping or straightening of the CB seam. **N.B.** It is generally better, after ascertaining that the correction required by the figure is possible (i.e. turnings permitting), *to do it first on the pattern*; the slacks can then be corrected by re-laying the pattern.

BASIC WIDTH DEFECTS

The length from the front fork point (F) to the back fork point (B) is basically taken as ¾ hip measurement but nowadays is generally less. This **basic width** of the pattern is reduced for *the closer-fitting style of slacks now in*

fashion, or for a *closer fit* on a slim (flat) figure, so that the proportion usually becomes ¾ hip measurement minus 4 or 5 cm, or possibly even tighter (e.g. in stretch fabrics).

While slim figures can have this basic width reduced, particularly when the *top leg fit* is required to be very tight, larger figures, and those with a prominent seat and very hollow waist, may need the full width equal to ¾ hips, or at least ¾ hips minus 2 or 3 cm. The general tendency in modern cutting, however, is to cut trousers tighter, i.e. shorter along the Basic line.

It may also sometimes be necessary to increase the basic width from F to B for various special purposes, e.g. in sports wear to allow for more 'stride' (skiing).

The fork points F and B can sometimes be changed slightly, i.e. projected more, or less, beyond the CF and CB lines. For a figure with a prominent seat, or generally big hips, it may be found necessary to add, i.e. *let out at point B*; a figure with a prominent abdomen—may require point F to come a little further out beyond the CF

FIG. 24/v

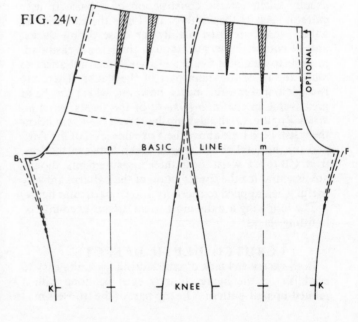

line. So the shape of the figure can to a certain extent influence *the position of the two points* (in relation to CF and CB lines) and thus affect also the *total basic width* (Fig. 24). **At the fitting** the defect shows as **tightness** (tight short creases) **in the crutch part**.

HIP AND WAIST WIDTH DEFECTS

Hip width is regulated mainly **at the side seams** which can be let out or taken in as required not only by the *size*, but also by the *shape* of the hips (e.g. prominent hip bone). The **waist** is controlled by **the darts**, including the one in the side seam. They may occasionally need re-arranging to suit the figure. From a fitting point of view it is generally not an advantage to have too many darts or deep darts in the back as it tends to overshape the figure, and contributes to the 'bagginess' of the back. More darts or 'pleats' (folds) in the front are now usually preferred (Fig. 24).

Darts should not be too long *to avoid tightening too much the part above the hip line*: checking width below their points is useful (see Check Measurements lower). Some looseness in the waist may be accepted to provide a little 'spring' for the CB seam, i.e. to allow the back waist to slip down when sitting. The CB seam can thus be kept shorter, i.e. straighter.

DEFECTS IN THE LEG PART

Creasing of the leg part is due mainly to **excessive tightening** (particularly on a figure which is not very suitable for trousers), and in most cases this cannot be avoided, so that when tight slacks are fashionable it is often disregarded.

When overfitted, the **inner leg seams** become **too curved** and the pattern then is too 'open' in the leg part (Fig. 25).

Up to a point it is possible to correct this by bringing the leg seams closer together. Let out at the bottom of the inner leg seam and reduce by the same amount on the outer seam, running off the two lines at crutch and hip level.

ADDITIONAL CHECK MEASUREMENTS

The high Hip measurement is useful, particularly in larger sizes. If this check measurement differs little from the full hips, this indicates that the figure is thick right through or has a prominent abdomen, and precautions must be taken to ensure that the pattern is wide enough on this level (10–12 cm below the waist). Width can be added right through in the side seam, and the Waist darts kept small and short.

The total crutch length measurement when applied to the *combined CB and CF seams* (Fig. 26) soon establishes whether the crutch fit is likely to be correct or not. It must be noted, however, that the length—if insufficient—can be increased in the pattern or at the fitting in several ways: by adding to the 'depth of crutch', i.e. letting down from the waist; by lengthening the CB seam, i.e. giving it a more sloping 'seat angle', *if* the figure *appears to need it*; and by extending the basic line, i.e. letting out at B or F. Which of these adjustments is called for, the fitting should establish: in a more serious case all three may be required. The reverse, of course, would be done to shorten the total crutch length, more often by reducing the Depth of crutch i.e. by pulling up from the waist, but sometimes, according to the shape of the figure, also by shortening B–F line (tightening between the legs) or straightening the CB seam. This must be a practical solution *depending on the fit required by the figure*: the check measurement merely points to the problem.

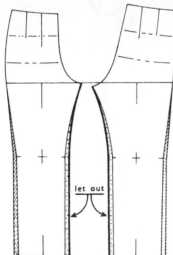

FIG. 25/v

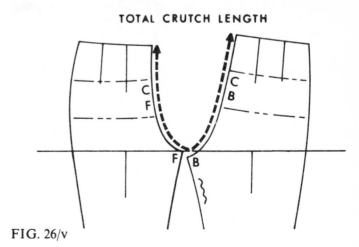

TOTAL CRUTCH LENGTH

FIG. 26/v

CHAPTER SIX | **THE PROBLEMS OF THE ONE-PIECE DRESS**

The pattern with the bodice and skirt cut in one, **without a join at the waist**, is used for a big variety of garments: it appears in underwear, in all kinds of overalls and dressing gowns, in short and long coats, as well as in a big range of dress styles. There are certain periods in fashion when the One-piece dress foundation acquires particular importance because so many designs, simple and elaborate, are based on it. It is particularly at such times that a few *special fitting problems* have to be considered.

All the general defects and fitting adjustments examined in earlier chapters, such as those connected with the set of the shoulder, the balance, the sleeve and neckline fit, etc., apply of course to these styles as well. There are however a few additional difficulties, mainly connected with *silhouette* and *hang*, which are characteristic of this type of dress and which will be considered in this chapter.

There are two main varieties of one-piece garment: **the Straight and the Shaped**. The Shaped includes the Princess cut. Their *special* fitting problems are not necessarily the same: in fact, they are more likely to be different. The shaped pattern, whether **close-fitting or semi-shaped**, and whether consisting of many or only two sections, depends for its good fit mainly on *the way it outlines or moulds the figure*; in the Straight One-piece dress the most important thing is a *good hang from the shoulders*.

THE STRAIGHT ONE-PIECE DRESS

Basically, this is a very simple pattern consisting of a back and front with two side seams, and possibly a CB seam. It may of course appear in a big variety of styles and be very 'cut up' by yokes, panels and other fancy lines and sections, which may or may not present special problems to the fitter. However, the many permutations of details and any complications connected with them can be considered only as *special difficulties of a particular style*, to be solved according to circumstances.

The basic foundation itself, however, **has a few problems of fit** which it is advisable to consider right from the pattern stage. It is precisely because of its simple structure that it is so important that it should have *a good line*. As with skirts, which depend so much for their line on a correct hang from the waist, this pattern must hang correctly from the shoulders to give **the required fashion silhouette**. This is the most characteristic feature of a well-cut One-piece dress.

The hang from the shoulders is very much controlled by the position of the surplus fullness, as has already been demonstrated in some of the Modelling exercises in Chapter One. According to whether the floating surplus fullness is well distributed, or moved largely (if not entirely) into the hem, or concentrated mainly in the neck-

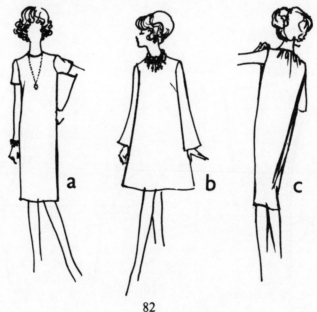

a   b   c

82

line and shoulders, the dress will **hang quite straight**, in a more or less vertical line (sketch *a*) or **swing away from the figure** (sketch *b*) or appear **to go in towards the hem** (sketch *c*): these are the different fashion lines of the Straight One-piece dress, and they were all popular in recent years (the 'shift', the 'tent' dress and the 'sack'). In the first instance, therefore, the pattern must *interpret the line correctly*, for later adjustments on the figure may be quite difficult.

The three patterns (only the backs are shown) corresponding to the three silhouettes of the sketches are given in Figs. 1, 2 and 3, and show the surplus fullness in different positions according to the 'line' of the style. They suggest how to deal with any **necessary adjustments of the line** at the fitting, or with any replanning of the pattern after a fitting. Broken lines show additional details such as darts or extra fullness which a pattern may or may not need, while dot-dash lines indicate essential turnings for possible alterations.

A dress which swings out too much at the hem can be reduced in width only a little from the side before creases (diagonal folds) appear from below the shoulder blade, running into the side seams. Therefore, for a bigger correction, it is necessary, after undoing the whole side seam, to raise the back into the armhole (1–1·5 cm) and then move the resulting armhole fullness into the shoulder or neckline (the same can be done for the front where,

however, an underarm dart is more often used). For such an adjustment to be possible, suitable turnings must, of course, be available. This lifting of the side seam into the armhole (increasing darts at the top) reduces the width at the hem and so *straightens the line of the dress correctly*, without risk of further complications. **When dealing with the pattern** this simply means reducing the slash (Fig. 2) which runs below the wholly or partly closed shoulder dart into the hem, and again increasing the dart at the top. **A dress which goes in too much at the hem** (the sloping-in line) can, **at the fitting**, be made to stand away more from the figure by transferring some of the shoulder dart fullness into the hem, through the armhole and down the side seam (exactly as in the Modelling exercises V and IX, though only small amounts), and then letting out the side seam at the hem (this is of course the reverse of the method described above). **To adjust the pattern** a slash is made below the shoulder dart into which *some* of the dart fullness is transferred.

It is useful to repeat again that letting out or taking in the hem width at the side seam is limited to a comparatively small amount, unless the dress has originally been cut with a very 'sloping-out' side seam—never a very successful cut. Correcting only from the side seam soon produces diagonal drags and does not affect sufficiently the 'line' of the dress as a whole, i.e. the middle part of the dress hardly alters and cannot be made to cling more

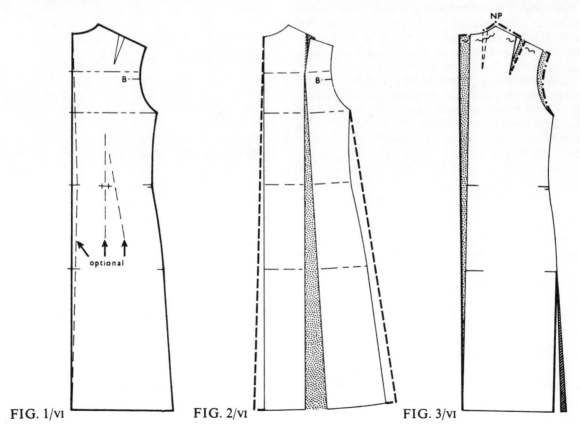

FIG. 1/VI   FIG. 2/VI   FIG. 3/VI

or to detach itself from the figure, as the case may be, unless the surplus fullness is brought into operation as well.

It is clear that such corrections of the line of the dress are more easy to obtain by **re-planning the pattern** and any extra addition of width for style down CF/CB (see Figs. 2 and 3), found excessive at the fitting, can always be adjusted best on the flat, re-outlining the corrected pattern within the turnings available.

Before leaving the subject of 'correct line', it is necessary to mention **the different shapes of figure** and how they affect the hang of a straight dress.

The line of a dress is not only a matter of fashion, i.e. of correct style interpretation; nor is it just a question of becomingness, when some details, e.g. hem width, may be regulated by what suits an individual person. The shape of the figure—if not average—can also influence the hang of a dress, as the following examples will show:

A very round-shouldered and stooping figure, fitting a straight dress, may show any of the relevant bodice defects already discussed in Chapter Two, but in addition, the dress would probably also *hang badly*, with the *back pulled up and standing away at the hem*. For the dress (irrespective of its design) to hang correctly, it will require a more sloping-in line (similar to Fig. 3), with more fullness or ease concentrated in the top and the NP and upper part of shoulder let out.

A figure with a prominent seat or a sway-back posture would probably look better in a straight One-piece dress if a little fullness were transferred in the back from the top into the hem, not to swing out the back for style effect, but just enough to follow the shape of the figure.

A figure with a very prominent bust requires a deeper bust dart often just to pull in the front below the waist.

A figure with a prominent abdomen would certainly need at least a little of the dart fullness *moved into the hem* to provide ease for the middle part of the front.

Thus, unless the figure is reasonably straight, the special requirements of its silhouette may have to be considered and the line of the dress adjusted accordingly.

A few special cases must also be mentioned when some of the surplus dart fullness is moved into the front hem to swing it out more: this may be done for instance to the front of a long One-piece dress (for better width distribution and easier walking), or to the front edges of a coat (to make them hang closer together when moving). However, this is usually incorporated in the pattern rather than done at the fitting.

Assuming, therefore, that a correct line has been achieved in the One-piece dress, either by fitting or preferably by correct designing of the pattern, there remain a few more specific problems of fit to be mentioned.

As the hang of the One-piece dress depends so much on the surplus fullness—its position and amount—it will be easily understood that in the back, for instance, the shoulder-blade dart (or equivalent easing) plays an im-

portant part in controlling the fit and must never be overlooked or ignored (in the front the Bust dart is too obvious to need stressing).

The shoulderblade dart in loose-hanging straight styles is generally used to its maximum depth and is often even increased slightly. This is done particularly for round-shouldered figures and for styles with a slightly 'sloping-in' line.

Letting out at the Neck point (NP) is another adjustment which one has to make fairly frequently in One-piece dresses (more often in the back only). The weight of a loose-hanging garment, whether coat or dress, is very

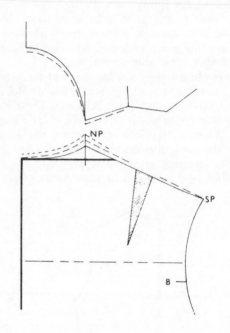

FIG. 4/VI

much centred on this point (NP) and since so many figures are at least slightly round shouldered, tightness at NP, with possible pulling up of hem, occurs very easily.

The letting out at back **NP** does not necessarily mean that the whole of the back neckline must be raised. The back neckline would normally be affected if the **NP** were raised to 2·5 cm or more *above the CB level* (see top dotted line in Fig. 4); whether it will actually be necessary to alter it for an *individual* shape of neck will be shown by the fitting.

Diagonal drag or creases into side seam, when not caused by roundness of back, prominent shoulder blade or bust (this, it is presumed, would already have been corrected earlier when fitting a bodice to the shape of the figure), are probably due either to slight tightness at NP or more likely, to **tightness of the side seam at hip level**. This applies, of course also to *shorter* straight garments as overshaping of side seams, when it is not done with a correct 'change of line' (i.e. moving of surplus fullness) as described earlier, soon brings in this defect.

Creasing in the hollow of the back waist is probably the most usual defect one encounters when fitting One-piece dresses, and when it is slight and seen mainly when the figure is in motion, it can be ignored. It occurs on all 'sway-back' figures—young and old, large and small—

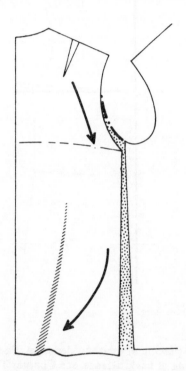

FIG. 5/VI

on those with a prominent seat and on all those with a bad posture. It is something that one comes across so frequently in all straight styles, particularly in dresses, that it may be advisable in order to avoid this defect to take the precaution of adjusting the pattern in advance, before cutting the material. A suitable pattern adaptation is shown in Figs. 6, 7 and 8.

At the fitting it is necessary to undo the side seam and then to move the back just over 1 cm down the front while letting out the seam slightly *to detach the back from the hips* (Fig. 5), in fact, exactly as was done for the bodice in Chapter Two (Fig. 22). Once the clinging of the dress to the hips is released and it no longer 'catches' on the CB, the *apparent* excess length will work itself down and the waist creases disappear. This was demonstrated in the Modelling Exercise VI-A (Method I) which gives the basis for all adjustments of this type with a *minimum* increase in

hip width. Re-shape the armhole in its lower part and level the hem from the ground.

In the front the problem does not arise quite so often, but if it does, and there is tightness *below waist and hips* (e.g. in the case of overdeveloped thigh muscles), the same procedure could be adopted to remove creases and untidy fullness between waist and top of legs. More frequently however, and always if the defect is more serious, the correction is done by *transferring part of the Shoulder dart into the hem*, and simply *swinging out* the whole front for greater ease in moving.

Adjusting the pattern before a fitting to avoid the above defect is advisable when it is clear that the figure is likely to need it. In fact, **in the back the adjustment can be incorporated in the pattern** just as it is generally done for loose-hanging (Boxy) jackets and coats, to improve the hang of the back.

There is more than one way of doing this in a pattern, but the most usual method is shown in Fig. 6 where the CB of the pattern is shortened by a 1 + cm horizontal dart

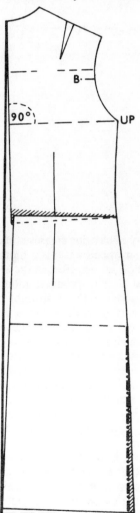

FIG. 6/VI

(or overlap) running off to nothing at the side seam. The CB line is then drawn a little further out, connecting the CB nape point with the jutting out CB seam at the hem. A similar effect would have been obtained by simply sloping out the CB line (as in Fig. 23, Chapter Two), but with a constantly changing hem length in dresses it is not so easy to assess the amount of the slope at the hem.

There are **other ways of pulling up the back to clear** waist creases, but these depend on style lines. Thus in a style with a back yoke it is possible to pull up the CB into the yoke line and, by shortening, prevent it clinging too much to the figure.

Finally, it must be mentioned that sometimes a back may appear loose and creased *as if it were too long*, which in actual fact it is: this is a question of **wrong balance** at the top, possibly caused by excessive raising of NP or

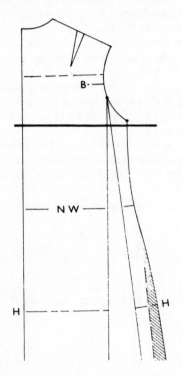

FIG. 7/VI

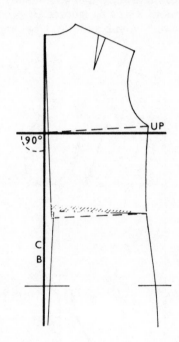

FIG. 8/VI

Another way of clearing creases at the waist (or simply preventing their appearance) is a more definite 'flaring' from the armhole, as described in the Modelling Exercise VI-A, Method II. This produces more width round the hips and is used mainly in straight coats and 'Boxy' jackets, and so is generally incorporated in the pattern (Fig. 7). It gives more width under the armhole ('the drape' fold) which is of course quite acceptable for many dressmaking styles as well (straight dress jackets, over-blouses, and even some pouched styles). On the whole, the first method is the one that is suitable for One-piece dresses, as it achieves a similar result of *detaching the back of the dress from the figure* (and so clearing the creases) without adding so much width round the hips and in the hem.

Fig. 8 shows, however, that in both cases the UP is raised above the former X–SG level and therefore must be brought down to it when joining the Front UP: this is precisely what causes the swinging out of the CB and releases the tightness.

forward placing of the shoulder seam. For **correction**, i.e. **shortening of back balance**, see Chapter Two, Fig. 16.

A **loose-hanging straight dress** can be made to cling to the figure just enough **to remove the excess fullness** but without losing its easy-fitting line. To achieve this *without getting a close or even semi-shaped fit* is not always easy, and **the basic waist darts**, placed *up and down the figure* are not the most suitable ones to use because, unless quite insignificant, they tend to overshape the dress: they follow too closely the curves of the figure. Small darts and dart-seams placed in less usual positions, which can suppress excess fullness *without following too much the shape of the figure*, are often used in a variety of ways—mainly slanted.

The diagonal dart below the shoulder blade and similar darts (dart-seams) running from neckline to bust and from bust down towards the side seams, are examples of this *technique of removing unwanted fullness* without losing the all-over easy fit of the style. At a fitting it is often necessary to make use of such additional darts.

THE SHAPED ONE-PIECE DRESS

This can be either a simple type of 'Sheath' dress, just back and front with two or three seams, or a Princess style consisting of several sections. Since the fitted **Sheath dress** relies for its close fit mainly on **vertical darts above and below the bust and shoulder blade**, it more or less follows the shaping of the classical Princess cut, omitting only the actual seams in which the darts of that pattern are enclosed.

The Princess dress can be varied in many different ways, by changing the number of seams, width of panels, fullness at the hem, by adding yokes or other fancy lines, etc. Whatever the style details, however, the problems of fit are much the same in all Shaped One-pieces dresses, the aim being always **to achieve a more or less close fit** to the figure.

On the whole the Princess dress is not a difficult pattern to fit because, in principle at least, it can be adapted to almost any shape of figure: the basic seams are in the best position for this purpose. However, whether it is always the best policy to follow very closely the shape of a figure is a different matter: in some cases it may not be an advantage to outline the figure too much. This, rather than the actual fit, may sometimes present a problem to the fitter, who will then consider the question of 'becomingness' before that of 'perfect fit'.

Seams and darts. In principle the more seams there are, the easier it is to follow the shape of the figure.

When there are only two other seams in addition to the side seam, i.e. one on the CB and one on the CF (the 4-gore Princess style), additional waist darts may be required between the seams for a tighter fit, particularly on figures with a small waist. It is not advisable to take in, i.e. *curve*, the seams too much, as this may produce horizontal folds at the waist, the seams in this case being too far apart. However, the exact effect of seam tightening or of extra darts can always be judged best at the fitting.

The classical Princess dress which has either 6 or—with CB and CF seams—8 gores, may also sometimes need an *additional front waist dart*, often a slanted one, placed between the bust Panel seam and the side. This helps to avoid curving the Panel seam too much over the bust, where *overshaping is often considered unsuitable* (either for the style or for the figure), or simply unattractive. Additional back waist darts are not often used, particularly when there is a CB seam.

A good balance between the seams and any additional darts used mainly to prevent overshaping of seams, must be left to the judgement of the fitter.

Fitting lines and style lines of the panel seam. As already explained in the drafting of the pattern of a Princess dress, one of the edges of the panel seam is the fitting line, and the other the style line. **The fitting line** adjusts the fit to the contour of the figure. **The style line** establishes the exact shape of the panel according to the design.

It is on the *outer edge* of the panel seam, over or under the bust and shoulder blade, that the main fitting, i.e. letting out or taking in is done. The other edge is altered only when the shape or *style of the panel* must be changed, either because it was wrongly interpreted in the pattern, or because it does not suit the person fitted. This obviously does not happen often, as a design is generally judged from this point of view at an earlier stage, in fact when the style selection is made.

The side seams and the CF and CB seams are generally used less for fitting than the panel seams, because they deal mainly with the *size* (which should be more or less correct) rather than with the *shape* of the figure; but some adjustment can always be made here, if found necessary.

Hem width will have been allowed as required by the style but, if it is to be changed, one must remember whether, in the pattern, it had been added *evenly all round* or, according to the design, *distributed unevenly*, e.g. in a long Princess dress with more hem width in the back. This must be taken into account in any correcting. On the other hand, hem width can be added or reduced in the seams at a fitting just where it appears to be necessary not only according to the style, but sometimes also according to the posture of the figure. Neither definite rules nor advice can be given on this subject as tightness or fullness of hem is very much a matter of style, fabric, prevailing fashion, and personal preference.

In a **tight sheath dress** the tightness of the hem will generally be tested at the fitting to see to what extent it permits freedom of movement, bearing in mind that a tall, 'striding' figure with long legs will need more hem width for walking.

Problems of darts. The bigger or deeper a dart, the longer it has to be to run off neatly at the point. Short darts, when deep, tend to 'poke' at the end, and may be difficult to blend into the surface of the garment, particularly in some fabrics which do not press or shink easily. At a fitting, therefore, one should remember that when a dart has to be increased for closer fit, *it should be possible to make it longer*. This becomes particularly important when the original dart is already quite a big one.

In the Princess dress or any style with panels and extra seams there are few difficulties because the main darts are enclosed in the seams and so, when increased in depth, they can easily be made longer. With close fitting sheath dresses it is more difficult because, in tightening the fit, not only will the deeper darts have to be lengthened, possibly to the detriment of the general appearance, but there may be the added trouble of dealing with their pressing.

Yet another difficulty which may arise when darts have to be increased to tighten the waist is the all-over unwanted **tightening of the whole garment**, as the lengthening of deeper darts may cause too much bust and hip width to be lost. This is often quite a serious problem which, however, must be left to the judgement and experience of the fitter. The point to remember is that a bigger waist dart will make the garment tighter *above and below* as well, with such possible consequences as the 'riding up' of the whole dress and the formation of more creases and folds than ever before. The greatest care must be taken at the fitting that no sign of this appears when darts are pinned tighter on the figure, for later machining of the seams may exaggerate the tightness.

THE SEMI-SHAPED DRESS

There is little that can be added about the fitting of semi-shaped dresses, for they are just more easy fitting variants of close fitting styles. Their cut follows the same principles and is based, either on the Princess line or on a looser, less darted, sheath dress. Their fitting problems are therefore similar though simpler.

Because of the easier all-over fit, some of the difficulties mentioned in connection with tight fitting styles do not exist. The darts are always smaller, and there is much less danger of any overshaping trouble.

The only thing to remember about these dresses (which at times are more fashionable than either the Straight or the close fitting ones) is that they generally have *a distinctive line of their own* and must not look like badly-fitted tight styles. Their line *indicates* the silhouette of the figure without moulding it; yet it can do this in different ways: and there are various important *fashion details of fit*—such as slight 'hugging' of the hips or extra tightening above or below the bust, etc., which must be very carefully observed and correctly reproduced in the pattern.

A good cut, based on careful fashion observation is therefore most important in these styles.

CHAPTER SEVEN | KIMONO, RAGLAN, DROP-SHOULDER FITTING

When dealing with a Kimono, a Raglan or a Drop-shoulder style it is important to be sure that to begin with the construction of the original pattern is correct, for here one cannot rely upon achieving a big change at a fitting, as in the case of an ordinary bodice. Where the sleeve and bodice are *cut in one*—either completely, as in a kimono, or partly as in a raglan or drop-shoulder—adjustments at a fitting are always more difficult and require great care and a good understanding of the construction of the pattern.

THE KIMONO

As already stated, a bodice with set-in sleeves is much more easy to control from the point of view of fit than a bodice with sleeves cut in one, for in the latter case any adjustment to the bodice part will naturally affect the sleeve part also, whether the sleeve needs to be altered or not. For example, if the shoulder of the kimono has to be tightened at SP, the sleeve must be replanned from a new, i.e. lower SP point, and this brings it lower down the underarm, with the result that the underarm is shortened and the kimono may be less comfortable. Thus, while one part is adjusted, the fit of another can easily be upset.*

Basically, of course, the kimono is a primitive pattern which is not expected to 'fit' in the strict sense of the word: it has a 'draping line' of its own which is attractive and generally liked, but which certainly looks better on some figures than on others. If it happens to be not very becoming to a figure, it is difficult to improve its fit. For instance, a figure with fairly square shoulders, upright carriage and not very prominent bust will generally look well in a kimono; whereas a stooping figure, with sloping shoulders or one with a very big and low bust, will not show off the draping line of the kimono to advantage.

Admittedly, the modern kimono presents a choice of many different 'lines' (or silhouettes), from the loose draping dolman to the close fitting, figure-moulding dress bodice, and there are many refinements of cut and fit (e.g. elaborate gussets) which were unknown in the primitive version, But this does not necessarily make it a suitable pattern for every type of figure or for every type of garment. It may, for instance, be found to be quite becoming for someone as a coat of the 'dolman' variety, yet not very flattering as a close fitting dress style. This is

*For the basic construction of a kimono see Chapter Two of *More Dress Pattern Designing*

a fact that must always be borne in mind.

When dealing with an individual figure, a preliminary choice must often be made as to which sloping line of the kimono sleeve to use for the correct style effect or, sometimes, for the shape of the figure. Once this choice has been made, it is not easy to alter the slope at the actual fitting. It can only be done by complete re-planning or adjustment of the pattern after the fitting. Thus, *some of the fitting of a kimono has to be done on the flat* at a later stage.

Although it appears logical that a well fitting bodice block should provide the best foundation for a good kimono adaptation, this does not necessarily work out in practice because of the special nature of the kimono cut: a carefully fitted bodice block does not always give the best results when adapted to a kimono pattern. In fact, the good balance or *hang of a kimono* may even be upset by too much *individual fitting* of the original bodice block, so that the final result is not as good as when a stock size kimono block is used. It is therefore generally a good plan **to use an average kimono block** nearest in size to the measurements of the figure, and to learn to introduce into the pattern such **adjustments** as may appear to be **essential for the figure**. This could of course be done at a fitting, when any shortcomings of the stock size block would be obvious (e.g. insufficient height of back for a stooping figure); but on the whole, most of the necessary adjustments would be done on the flat, *either before or after the fitting*, to ensure that **the correct balance of the original is maintained**.

Thus, to sum up, some corrections, namely those referring to details of style rather than to the basic construction, can be made at a fitting; more important alterations, involving the actual structure of the pattern (e.g. squaring of shoulder) are made later on the flat when, *on the basis of observations made at the fitting*, the pattern may have to be re-planned and outlined again on the material.

CORRECTIONS MADE AT THE FITTING

Whether a kimono has been adapted from an individually fitted bodice block or from the nearest stock-size kimono pattern, possibly with a few adjustments made in advance to suit the figure, the following **simpler alterations can be made at the fitting** without fear of unbalancing the whole pattern and of losing its original basic coherence.

Width of back neckline. If, in drafting the kimono, a S1.CB was used, it must be remembered that this adds to the width of the back neckline: any such extra width should be kept in the neckline, at the fitting by pinning it out, and later by dealing with it as suitable for the style, but usually simply by easing before finishing off the neckline. With the extra width pinned out, the width round the back of the neck must be just right: it must not be allowed to 'spread' into the shoulder part and to *push the whole shoulder out* (down the arm).

Bust width. This can sometimes be reduced by 0·5–1 cm on the double mainly, but not necessarily always, in the smaller sizes. It is important, however, to know **which underarm seam was used** in the kimono adaptation: **the inner,** which is taken from the UP of the original bodice block (i.e. the level of the bust line—see Fig. 1) or **the**

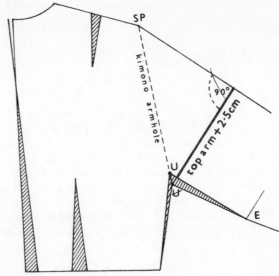

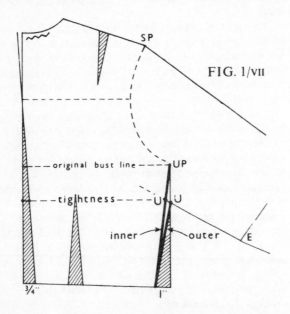

FIG. 1/VII

the basic kimono sleeve, can be reduced, if this appears to be necessary or more becoming, provided the loose 'draped' effect of its underarm is preserved.

In connection with this there is a useful controlling measurement which often helps to prevent overfitting of kimono sleeves at the top (near the Top arm muscle): a line taken at right angles to the Top Line of the kimono *back* and touching point U (Fig. 2) should measure half the Top Arm measurement 2·5 cm as a minimum.

On the whole, beyond these minor adjustments, the underarm is best left alone, as there is a very delicate balance between *the slope of the sleeve* and its width, which can be easily upset if the bust or sleeve width are tampered with too much.

The shoulder-sleeve seam or the top line of the kimono. This combined seam does not always run as it should on

outer, which runs from the crossing of the sleeve line with the vertical (construction) side seam. The *inner* seam already represents a *width reduction suitable for most smaller figures* and any further reduction in width must be done with the utmost care. Reductions of more than 0·5 cm on the double are generally done only on the *outer* side seam, which is often more suitable for larger figures.

Much depends also on how much was lost on the *slanting of the CB* and, of course, on the required tightness of the style, which may or may not be suitable for some figures.

N.B. Excessive tightening of bust width may cause a kimono to 'ride up', as will be explained later.

Sleeve width. Here again only a very small loss of the **basic sleeve width** is possible and then only if the style is expected to be close fitting (e.g. a short or long tight sleeve). On the other hand, a **kimono dolman sleeve,** which is already much wider in the top part (at point U) than

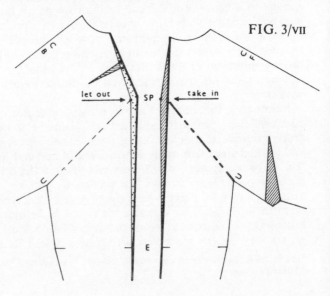

FIG. 3/VII

the figure, i.e. **down the middle of the shoulder**. It must be remembered that an extra addition to the height of the back part has already been made in the construction of the kimono pattern when dividing the sleeve *unevenly* between the front and the back: this is done precisely to ensure a better position of the sleeve seam on the figure. Nevertheless, **if the seam appears to 'fall back'** too much at SP (and possibly also at NP), one can undo it some way beyond SP and repin it on the figure **letting out on the back and taking the same amount off the front** (Fig. 3). This will produce a bigger 'bulge' at SP in the back and a flatter (straighter) line on the front edge of the seam (particularly if NP is *not moved* forward as well). The line of the seam should be made to run smoothly into the sleeve seam (possibly 'eased' at back SP).

It is not often that the combined shoulder-sleeve seam needs to have more than this done to it; but if it does, in an

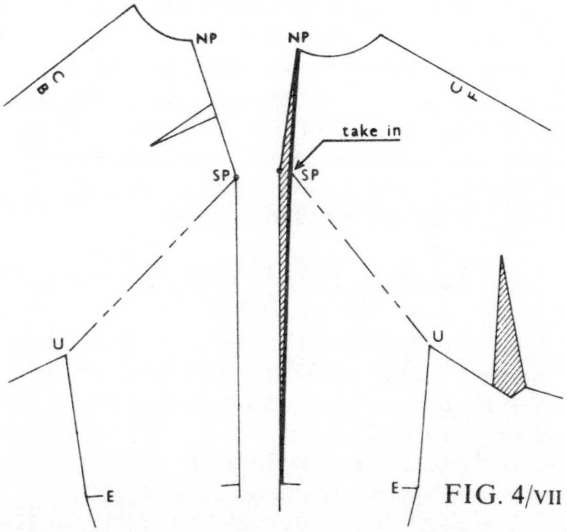

(b) If the above is not sufficient one can also undo the shoulder at NP and let out 0·5 cm on both back and front (Fig. 5) which also helps to 'tighten' shoulder at SP by giving the whole shoulder section a bigger slope (see Shoulder Defects in Chapter Two). The neckline may need a slight adjustment.

Both these are only minor corrections, quite easy to carry out at an actual fitting. If found insufficient, e.g. when fitting an *average* kimono pattern on a figure with very sloping shoulders, further shoulder tightening should be done on the flat, as it involves an adjustment of the underarm part of the pattern and *the lowering of point U* (see Fig. 9 lower).

All this does not necessarily apply to a **deep dolman sleeve** where more tightening of shoulder at SP may be done because of the existing *underarm depth*, and where the shoulder tightness can therefore be adjusted more

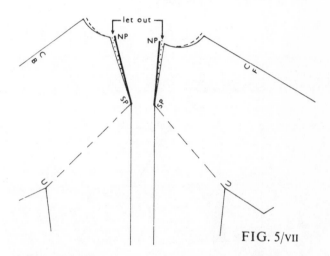

FIG. 4/VII

FIG. 5/VII

exceptional case (e.g. when it is too far back on a very stooping figure), it is best *to replan the line on the pattern after the fitting* and to tack the garment up again with the correction (see lower). A few pins or chalk marks can be used at the fitting to indicate the improved line.

Tightening of shoulder-sleeve seam for more sloping shoulder. If the kimono bodice sags badly in the 'armhole part', **the shoulder is too loose.** This may indicate a more fundamental correction, best attempted on the flat *after* the fitting, but in a minor case, the following can be tried out at once:

(a) Undo the shoulder part of the seam without touching NP (at least to begin with and take 0·5–1 cm off the front at SP (Fig. 4), which will flatten the front seam line; bring the back SP over to this point. In some cases it may be better for the shape of the line to take 0·5 cm *equally* off back and front. It will be remembered that in the construction of the kimono pattern 1 cm was allowed between the shoulder lines when joining sleeve to bodice: some or all of this is now lost in order **to tighten the shoulder at SP**.

easily at a fitting.

When fashionable or otherwise suitable, shoulder pads can be used to achieve much the same effect: by building up the shoulder itself a tighter fit at SP is obtained. The effect of shoulder pads should be tested at a fitting.

If the shoulder is *more square* (i.e. higher) than usual the shoulder fit of a kimono is better altered *on the flat* (see section 'Corrections made on the pattern').

Waist darts can be re-arranged at a fitting, if necessary, and also made bigger (deeper) or smaller. A warning must be given, however, that **excessive tightening of the waist darts** (which at one time was very fashionable) results in *longer* darts. These longer or higher darts may lead to over-fitting of the part just below the waist and round the bust (Fig. 1), with the result that the kimono bodice 'rides up' and the shoulder part becomes loose and stands away from the figure. The impression is that the shoulder needs tightening, i.e. taking in.

This is what fitters generally do as an *emergency correction* although the real cause of the trouble is not in the shoulder part at all, but in the waist.

The gusset—its position and length. It is important to establish **the correct position of the gusset line on the figure**. This line should be clearly marked (tacked) on the garment but not cut into before a fitting. The Gusset line (from U to G—see Fig. 6) must run *inside* the Kimono Armhole line (i.e. the line from U to SP), and must always allow for the full width of the Back and Chest measurements, without, however, exaggerating them. **At the fitting** it may be found that point G has to be moved in on the figure, i.e. towards CB/CF (seldom the other way round) to make the line U–G **slope more inwards**. Since the gusset in fact replaces the lower part of the armhole, the line U–G must always follow a direction which brings it as close as possible to the original bodice armhole.

If at the fitting of a kimono it is necessry to lose some bust width or sleeve width, which involves the **moving of point U further in**, the gusset line is, of course, **re-planned from this new position of point U**.

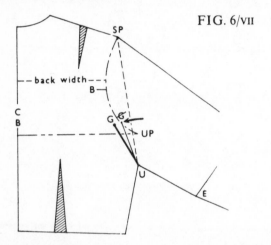

FIG. 6/VII

In some cases, generally in the closer fitting kimono sleeves, it may be necessary to indicate at the fitting an **upward lengthening of the gusset line** to release the sleeve more from the bodice part. In other cases the line U–G may be shortened in order *to conceal the gusset more under the arm*: this is likely to be suitable for the deeper underarm which gives a more draped effect.

It will be obvious that until the gusset line is cut and the lower part of the sleeve is released from the bodice, it may be difficult, particularly for a less experienced fitter, to obtain a clear idea of the fit of the kimono. Since it is not advisable to cut before a fitting, because of the need *to check the gusset line position*, it is not always easy to do much to the fit of a kimono at a first fitting.

Careful observations should, however, be made for possible adjustments later on the flat. A second fitting, with the gusset already inserted, is therefore generally useful.

All this applies mainly to the **basic, set-in gusset** which is an additional piece inserted into a slit or small opening. Not all kimono gussets are of this simple variety: there

are quite a number of **more complicated ones**, e.g. the strip gusset, the built-up gusset, etc. These are already part of the actual kimono construction, i.e. *part of the whole pattern*, and therefore do not involve any additional 'cutting into the garment' later. They have the advantage of showing the true fit of the kimono—as it will be in its final stage—at the first fitting. Should any correction be considered necessary, it will generally be found possible or easier to carry it out *after the fitting* by adjusting the whole pattern on the flat.

Style lines and details. These of course should be checked at a first fitting and many may be corrected at once. Whether it will be possible to correct all style details or whether some may have to be left for later re-planning on the pattern, depends on various circumstances. Simple details, such as the width or depth of a neckline, position of pockets, buttons and other additional trimming details can generally be adjusted at once. Other details, such as the depth of a yoke, width of a panel, shape of an inset piece, etc., are part of the style construction, i.e. of the pattern: any correction of these should be indicated by pins or chalk *to be adjusted later on the flat*. Fancy gussets are often closely connected with style lines and are then considered as part of the whole design rather than just as a means of releasing the sleeve.

CORRECTIONS MADE ON THE PATTERN

The following adjustments cannot be made easily on the figure at the fitting; so, *after careful observation of the defect on the figure*, they should be carried out on the flat by **altering the actual pattern**. It is obvious that when such a corrected pattern is outlined again on the already cut out material, one has to rely considerably on good turnings, without which it may be impossible to carry out alterations. It is therefore important to understand these problems if only **to know where useful turnings have to be allowed**.

The following are the most important adjustments which are best made on the flat:

Squaring the shoulder. The defect appears as diagonal creases below the shoulder (sketch), just like those which are observed in any sleeve where **the crown is too low**; but there may also be a feeling of **tightness over the shoulder bone** at SP. The defect may thus appear for two reasons: the combined shoulder-sleeve line passing *over SP is too short* either because the person being fitted has a *longer* than average shoulder or an over-developed top arm muscle; or because the shoulder is actually *squarer or higher than average*. The 'squaring' of a kimono thus covers both the problem of the *longer* and the *higher* shoulder and, since it requires a *lengthening of the top line precisely at SP* (and not at the wrist), an adjustment on the figure at the fitting is difficult.

N.B. When a square-shouldered silhouette is fashionable and shoulder padding is generally used, this adjust-

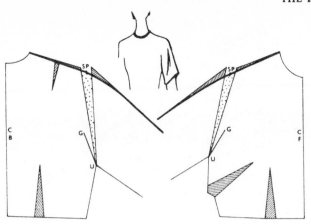

FIG. 7/VII

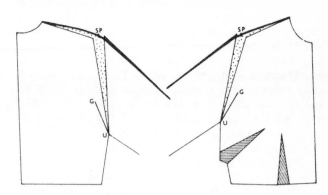

FIG. 8/VII

ment becomes essential for all kimono patterns (see also Chapter Three of 'More Dress Pattern Designing'—page 25).

Method: Cut the pattern from SP down to point U and open 2–3 cm (often more), on both back and front (Fig. 7). Judgement and experience will determine the amount to be added, and much will depend on whether the pattern had already been 'squared' at the preliminary stage. According to the shape of the shoulder **the new shoulder-sleeve line** can be drawn either **higher** or **lower**. When the shoulder is really square and tightness at SP was observed at the fitting, or when it must be padded to follow fashion, *extra height* can be added at SP (Fig. 8). When *loosening* of shoulder at SP is not considered desirable and the aim is mainly to *improve the hang of the sleeve* (i.e. remove creases) by extending its 'crown' part, the final top line can be made to pass below the top of the slash (as in Fig. 7).

It must be borne in mind that extra width—*the width of the slash*—appears across the back and the chest of the

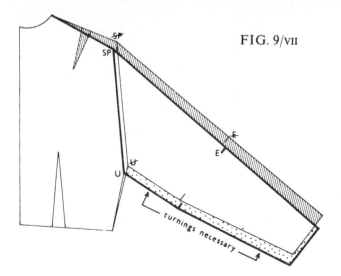

FIG. 9/VII

pattern: this however is easily distributed on a figure with square or even average shoulders. Only in some cases—on figures with very narrow chest and back width in proportion to the bust size—may this extra width be found superfluous: these, however, are usually figures with sloping shoulders for whom 'squaring' is neither necessary nor recommended.

Although the above adjustment is usually described as 'squaring the shoulder', it must be realized that the actual **sleeve part from SP down**, becomes **more sloping towards the wrist**, though without point U moving lower down the side seam. It is an important point to note, and it makes this adjustment useful in a variety of cases of kimono adaptation, e.g. when increasing the slant of the sleeve for certain special styles, such as the dolman-cape sleeve styles.

Sloping the shoulder. It has already been explained that a small *tightening of the shoulder at SP* which increases its slant, is possible at the fitting. In a more serious case it is best to re-plan the pattern on the flat **lowering SP** either equally on front and back (1–0·5 cm), or possibly more on the front than back (to improve the run of the shoulder seam); and **then to drop the equivalent amount on the side seam**, i.e. make point U come down lower in order to preserve the width of the sleeve. This would require the re-drawing of *the sleeve in a lower position* (Fig. 9), and would shorten the side seam. If a narrower sleeve is at all possible (test at the fitting), it is an advantage to lower point U a little less.

N.B. It must be mentioned again that this does not necessarily apply to the deep armhole styles, i.e. the dolman variety kimono, where point U need not be affected by the tightening of the shoulder.

It is useful to mention at this stage that, in fitting the kimono, 'sloping' or 'squaring' of the shoulder will be used more often or less often, not only because of *shape of figure*, but also because of prevailing fashion. For example, a **more sloping kimono shoulder**, i.e. **tighter at SP**, with the Top line almost straight, **helps a loose back** to hang better and might thus be preferred for styles without a join at the waist, particularly loose coats and dresses of the dolman variety. On the other hand, because a 'squared' kimono shoulder gives a better fit by helping to mould the shoulder bone, and remove creases from the top of the sleeve, it may be more in demand when closer fitting kimono styles are in fashion. Thus current fashion does influence the type of adjustment likely to be required, particularly if one bears in mind that the 'shoulder line' itself tends to become more square (e.g. even padded), or more sloping, according to changes in the fashion silhouette.

Changing the slant of the kimono sleeve. It is not often necessary, or even possible, to change the slant of the kimono sleeve, which involves a change *up or down* of point U; but should it be found necessary either to straighten (raise) or to slope the sleeve more, then—turnings permitting—this would of course be done not at the fitting but on the flat (Fig. 10). Like the much more frequent adjustment of the slant of the sleeves connected with the 'squaring' of the shoulder (Figs. 6 and 7) which is described above, it can be done only by replanning the pattern.

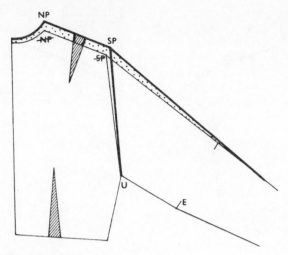

FIG. 11/VII

the 'armhole line' from SP down to U, *in the back only*: the front remains as it is. Open the slash 1–2 cm: this will slope the back part of the sleeve (as already explained in 'squaring'). Add the extra fullness of the slash to the existing back shoulder dart (as shown in Fig. 12), or ease it into seam between NP and SP. Re-draw the seam line. This is similar to the tightening of the back armhole in an ordinary bodice by increasing the shoulderblade dart; but since the correction involves the sleeve, which now *slopes more*, it should not be done unnecessarily, i.e. in cases where the creasing is only slight. Often a small pad will correct this defect sufficiently and is much safer and easier to use. N.B. It will be noted that in this case nothing was done to the front part of the sleeve except possibly taking it in a little at SP to bring the seam more forward.

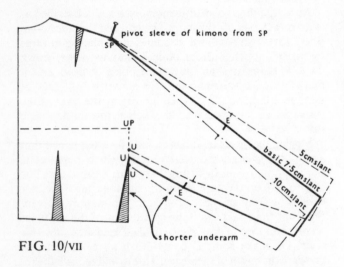

FIG. 10/VII

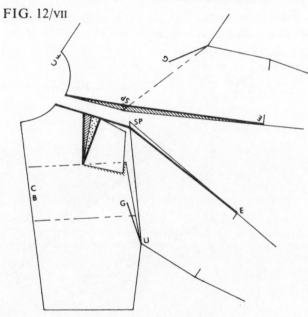

FIG. 12/VII

Adjusting the balance when the kimono tends to slip back off the shoulder. As was already explained, up to a point this can be corrected at the fitting, letting out a little on the back and taking up on the front. It is often, however, easier to do this on the flat and Fig. 11 shows the pattern after adding extra height to the back for a stooping figure. The corrected edge of the shoulder seam runs gradually into the sleeve seam. The front is reduced by the same amount (or sometimes a little less).

Pulling up the back 'armhole part' of a kimono is sometimes necessary on a figure with very round shoulders (protruding shoulder blades) and is really a problem of increasing the depth of the back shoulder dart. Cut along

Addition of bust width down CF(CB). On a figure with a very big bust the kimono sometimes appears tight across the front and yet seems loose under the arm. Add 0·5–1 cm down CF, as explained in Chapter Two for the usual bodice block (Chapter Two—Fig. 5). The width will either be retained in the front neckline (with the back neckline well pushed up and fitting correctly), or transferred into the bust dart (Fig. 13).

It is possible that occasionally a similar addition may be advisable for extra ease down CB, with the fullness retained in the neckline.

This adjustment will generally be accompanied by a slight *width reduction under the arm*.

Increasing the bust dart. The above paragraph already explains how the bust dart is increased (made deeper) *through the neckline* when more bust width is wanted across the front (Fig. 13). It is also possible to increase the bust dart by reducing a loose lower edge of the bodice, as explained in Chapter Two (Figs. 26 and 27).

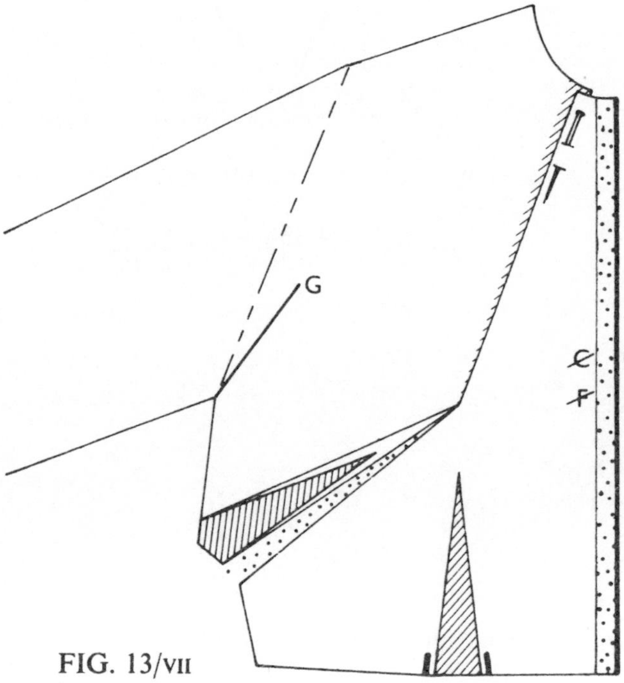

FIG. 13/VII

Gusset correction: if after checking the gusset position at the fitting, it is found that point G has to move further in, or if the bust width had been taken in at U, the gusset line U–G must be re-drawn in its **new position** before cutting on it and inserting the gusset. Any necessary **increase or decrease in the length** (height) of the gusset, and therefore of the slash, should be dealt with at the same time (see Fig. 6).

No rules or suggestions can be given for dealing with any fancy gussets or, in fact, with any fancy style lines: these would be judged and corrected according to circumstances, but always bearing in mind that the basic construction of the kimono should be tampered with as little as possible.

It is therefore useful to repeat at this stage the general warning that in spite of what may appear a considerable list of possible defects in a kimono, it is always advisable to avoid doing too much to the pattern and to accept a few creases as inevitable in a cut which is essentially that of a 'draped' garment. Even in its tightest fit (and this is where many troubles occur) it cannot achieve the smooth fit of an ordinary close fitting bodice.

As already stated, one of the objects of knowing something about possible defects is to understand where good turnings or inlays might be useful, e.g. on the underarm seam of a kimono sleeve, particularly near the wrist (as in Figs. 9 or 10), so that *a re-planned pattern* can be used on the material which is already cut out.

THE RAGLAN AND DROP-SHOULDER STYLES

Here the sleeve is only partly connected with the bodice and so the problems of fit are less numerous and complicated. They are mainly those of the shoulder section and the way it sets: the main part of the bodice and of the sleeve should have been checked by fitting the basic blocks.

THE RAGLAN

Assuming that *the construction of the raglan is correct*, the following few defects may still appear at a fitting:

Wrong balance. The shoulder section of the raglan sleeve must be placed on the figure so that it comes well up on the shoulder, with a slight *forward tilt* at NP. Any sloping back of the shoulder seam or dart from the middle, and any **slipping of the whole shoulder section towards the back** is wrong. The defect may be accompanied by an **untidy fit of the back armhole part** and indicates 'shortness' of back balance: the back of the bodice part is not deep enough (see Balance defects in Chapter Two). Theoretically, this should not happen if the original block had been carefully fitted and any lack of back depth rectified. In practice, however, a raglan style does tend to exaggerate this defect, and a reasonably satisfactory back may sometimes appear not quite deep enough when used with a raglan sleeve (e.g. on a very stooping figure).

To correct this balance defect is not particularly difficult, provided turnings are available at the top of the back, *below the shoulder section*. It can be done by letting out the top of the back at the fitting, or by re-planning the

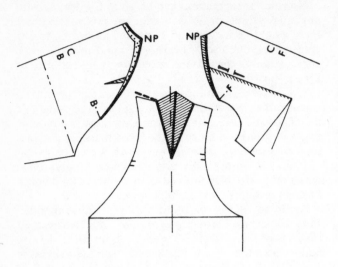

the other. Only a *small change* would be involved (0·5–1 cm), as any bigger displacement of the seam would spoil the shape of the shoulder section. This adjustment is sometimes combined with the previous one.

Tightness of shoulder. When a raglan is constructed from a bodice block which already provides a correct fit for a square or sloping shoulder, the raglan shoulder usually *adjusts itself* accordingly. It is important, however, to understand that the fit of a raglan at the shoulder end is actually regulated by **the depth of the dart at NP**, which is **bigger for a square shoulder** and **smaller for a more sloping one**.

Should it become necessary **to correct the tightness** of the shoulder **for a squarer effect** this will be achieved by **'squaring' the raglan** as shown in Fig. 16 (which increases the depth of the dart at NP) or, *in the case of a continuous*

FIG. 14/VII

pattern later, as shown in Fig. 14, **adding height to the back** and, if it appears necessary taking a little off the front, so that the shoulder section is shifted sufficiently towards the front.

The shoulder seam. Whether this is just **a dart or a seam**, it may sometimes be **badly placed on the shoulder for the figure**, too far back or, less often, too far forward. Assuming that the fit of the back, i.e. *the balance* is satisfactory, the seam (or dart) itself can be adjusted a little, as shown in Fig. 15, according to the shape of the shoulder, equally at SP and NP, or more at one end than

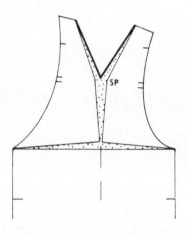

FIG. 16/VII

seam running into the sleeve, by simply letting out at SP, as for an ordinary shoulder. **At the fitting** a raglan can be squared more by **taking in the dart at NP**, i.e. making it *deeper*, and then letting out a little on the back and front raglan seams to compensate for the loss of width across the shoulder section.

For a very **sloping shoulder** the fit can be improved by re-planning the shoulder dart *on the flat* as shown in Fig. 17, i.e. making the dart smaller. **At the fitting** this is done by **letting out the dart at NP** and then reducing the shoulder section at the neck to its former width on the raglan seams. In an emergency (e.g. when there is no turning available), the shoulder can be taken up (tightened) at SP instead, after which the dart must be *lengthened into the sleeve*, to

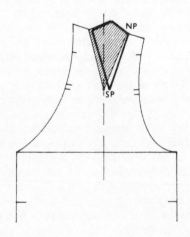

FIG. 15/VII

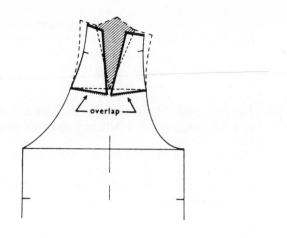

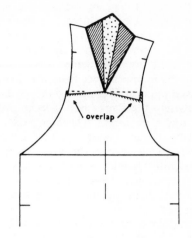

FIG. 17/VII   FIG. 18/VII

run off neatly. The same correction, of course, i.e. taking up at SP, would be used **for a seam** running into the sleeve.

The shoulder dart of the Raglan. With a few exceptions (e.g. in knitwear, or deep dolman styles), the raglan section has a deep dart (or equivalent seam) **to shape it to the angle of the shoulder.** To avoid making the dart too deep at NP, one can 'distribute' it a little by leaving some fullness (or ease) **in the raglan seams**, particularly in the front. However, should this be found inconvenient, and the excess fullness in the seams *difficult to deal with* (e.g. in some heavy fabrics, particularly in tailoring), it can always be eliminated in the pattern and transferred into the mid-shoulder dart instead, pinning out the 'ease' as shown in Fig. 18: the edges of the raglan section and of the bodice can then be *made to fit exactly*. If it is necessary to do this at the fitting, the 'ease' is pushed up towards the neck and into the dart, letting out a little on the raglan edges to compensate for loss of width through *dart increase.* Usually there is more to take out on the front seam than on the back.

It is important to understand that this fullness or ease—just like the ease in the crown of a sleeve—helps to *pull up the sleeve at the sides* and must not be pushed *down* into the armhole and taken out in the underarm sleeve seam if the hang of the sleeve is not to be spoiled by diagonal creases. Sometimes in dressmaking this fullness, instead of being eased in the raglan seams, can be suppressed in small darts taken at an angle to the shoulder seam and running off at or near SP. Some styles make this a feature of the design.

Some problems of the Raglan shoulder dart.

The shoulder dart must be quite deep if it is to mould the angle of the shoulder bone and *pull up the sleeve* well at the sides. As was already stated above, the ease in the raglan seams represents merely an attempt to 'distribute' the

dart and to reduce its depth at NP. The disadvantage of a very deep dart is that it is difficult to run it off neatly at the end (it pokes), and so it is often necessary to continue it beyond the shoulder point and down into the sleeve. This difficulty does not arise when the dart is replaced by a seam in which it is concealed; and that is why Top seams in raglan sleeves are so popular, and in fact almost a necessity in tailoring where the use of heavier fabrics makes easing and other fancy techniques unsuitable.

Therefore, if **flat Raglan seams** (without any ease) are preferred, one must be prepared to have to deal with a deeper shoulder dart, which often means that it has to be lengthened beyond the shoulder point (SP). This difficulty is reduced when the shape of the shoulder is square (high) or when shoulder padding is fashionable, or at least acceptable.

FIG. 19/VII

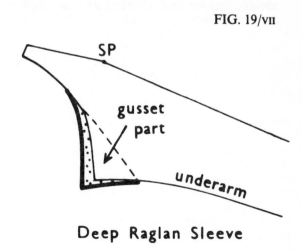

Deep Raglan Sleeve

N.B. There is a type of raglan—the deep dolman, usually cut on the kimono block—in which the shoulder dart can be kept smaller and part of its fullness pushed *down* into the extra wide armhole. The requirements of fit in this case are not the same: it is a 'draping' sleeve style, different in appearance from the classical raglan.

The gusset problem. When a raglan is of the low or deep dolman variety there may be a special problem of *insufficient underarm length*. The high raglan usually fits like an ordinary sleeve, even when the armhole, e.g. in a coat, is somewhat deeper. But a real deep raglan may sometimes pull too much when the arm is raised, and to release the strain may have to have the sleeve let out in the lower part of the armhole by increasing the 'gusset part' (Fig. 19).

The real dolman raglan should always be treated as a kimono as it involves all the kimono problems of fit.

A **sloping shoulder**, or an over-developed top arm muscle, would need a flatter, **less moulded fit** with a **looser edge**, which means a smaller 'dart' in the extended shoulder seam. The **correction of the pattern, reducing the dart**, is shown in Fig. 21. **At the fitting** it would mean letting out, i.e. loosening of the shoulder seam *beyond* SP. At the same time the seam may also need a little tightening, i.e. taking in *at the actual SP*, where the extra 1 cm allowed in the basic construction of the pattern may prove excessive for a sloping shoulder.

Since, in both cases, this involves a change in the lower edge of the cap, increasing or decreasing its length, *the sleeve has to be adjusted accordingly* in the lower part of the crown, below points F and B.

As the correction is usually small (1–2–2·5 cm), it is sometimes possible to avoid altering the sleeve by easing the cap edge into it or, the other way round, by easing the sleeve into the tightened cap. These are technical details which have to be decided according to circumstances—the style, fabric and the actual shape of the extension part.

THE DROP-SHOULDER STYLES

The most frequent and in fact almost the only trouble with these styles is a bad fit of the extended shoulder part, i.e. the 'cap' which may be **wrongly shaped for the curve of the shoulder**. In this connection there are two possible defects, both of which show mainly on *the lower edge* of the dropped shoulder, where the sleeve joins it.

Shoulder cap too flat: the extension is not sufficiently shaped to the angle of the shoulder bone and, being loose round the lower edge, the sleeve pulls it down into creases.

Shoulder cap over-shaped: here it is too close fitting to the top of the arm, i.e. tight round the lower edge, so that it impedes the raising of the arm and tends to ride up on to the shoulder.

In both cases the 'dart' *concealed in the extended shoulder seam* is wrong: it is either too small (in the first case) or too big for the curve of the shoulder.

A square shoulder, or a pronounced shoulder bone, may require an **increase of this dart**, so as to make the extension **mould the shoulder angle and top arm better**. Fig. 20 shows how to increase the 'dart' in the pattern, while at the same time lengthening slightly the shoulder seam at SP, as would actually happen *when letting out at SP on the figure* for a higher shoulder point.

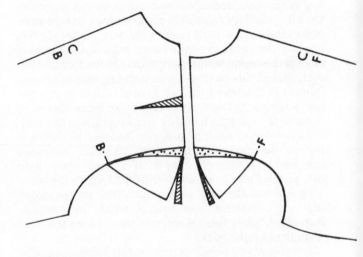

FIG. 20/VII

The other problem which sometimes arises with these styles is a problem connected with the design: according to the style, instead of the more usual crossing at B and F, **the extended shoulder section may cross the armhole above points B and F, or below these points**. In the first case there is no trouble for, as with the High raglan, the whole *lower part of the armhole remains untouched* and should therefore fit as the armhole of an ordinary sleeve. In the second an adjustment would be needed to release tightness on the Top arm and a 'pull' *under* the arm.

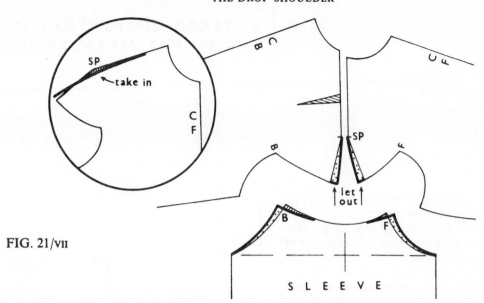

FIG. 21/VII

The low Drop-shoulder, even if it crosses the armhole only a little below B and F (e.g. 2·5 cm), is likely to cause **tightness when arm is raised** and this is corrected by **letting out the shoulder seam beyond SP**, as described above for reducing the 'dart' (Fig. 21). To release **the underarm 'pull'** which is also felt in these cases, **the sleeve must be let out at the top of its seam**, to gain both *width* and *height* and to be fitted into a *lowered armhole*. In **adjusting the pattern**, allow a bigger cap between the armhole and the 'drop-shoulder' sections (Fig. 22) *to loosen the lower edge of the cap*; then lower the armhole on the bodice part (1–2·5 cm), and finally adjust the sleeve: first increasing its top edge to fit the looser cap (see detail), then **raising the seam** as shown in Fig. 22, to reduce the underarm pull.

Thus a close fitting drop-shoulder style is possible only when the extension crosses the armhole at or above points B and F: with the lowering of the line and the consequent *reduction of the basic armhole*, the drop-shoulder gradually becomes in cut and fit more and more like a kimono.

The **real low drop-shoulder style** should always be cut on a Kimono block and so have a suitable 'gusset' worked into the sleeve part. If this is not done in advance, when planning the pattern, it may mean easing the shoulder and releasing the sleeve underarm considerably at the fitting. This indicates, of course, the importance of having suitable turnings in these parts as without these the correction would be difficult if not altogether impossible.

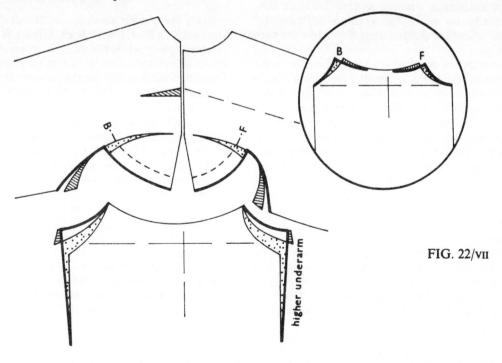

FIG. 22/VII

CHAPTER
EIGHT

PATTERN ADAPTATION TO INDIVIDUAL MEASUREMENTS

Stock size patterns are changed to other measurements (*a*) by grading or (*b*) by individual adaptation.

Grading deals with a systematic change of patterns from one stock size to other stock sizes either bigger or smaller. **Individual size adaptation** on the other hand deals with changes which make *a stock size pattern correct for an individual figure*. In the first case the pattern increases and decreases by definite regular proportions, following a Measurement Chart of *average sizes*, so that an *average* Bust 92 size increases to an *average* Bust 96 size or decreases to an 88 size. In the second case the pattern is changed in such a way that the resulting measurements correspond to those of *a particular figure*, in fact so that the pattern *fits this figure*.

GRADING

Grading is quite a big subject and this is not the place to deal with it in detail. It is, in fact, a technique of the wholesale manufacturing trade and is not concerned with problems of individual fit. The purpose of grading is to convert a stock size pattern into another in the quickest possible way consistent with accuracy, so as to avoid the necessity of drafting a separate pattern for each size. There is really no place for grading in 'bespoke' dressmaking where the pattern must be correct for each individual figure.

There are different ways of grading according to the requirements of the class of trade, the sizing charts followed (these vary considerably), and the actual production methods used. Some practical methods of grading, e.g. the 'shifting method', are particularly suitable for mass production: here the pattern, usually made in thick paper, is moved up and down, right and left, to obtain regular increases (decreases) at the different points, often covering in this way a big range of sizes. Manipulating the pattern to obtain these changes correctly is, of course, a special skill of a 'wholesale' pattern grader.

Most methods of grading make use of a network of **grading lines** to ensure that the basic structure of the pattern is not upset when the necessary increases and decreases are made at the various points. These grading lines are always either **horizontal** or **vertical**. They can also be distinguished as **primary** and **secondary**, the

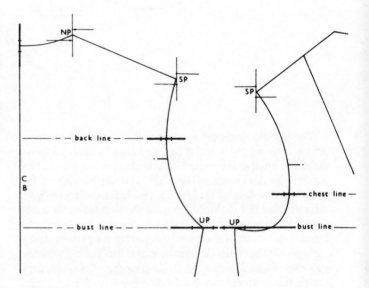

FIG. 1/VIII

primary being a continuation of the draft construction lines, such as Bust, Chest, Back, Hips, CB, CF lines (Fig. 1—thick lines), while the secondary are *additional lines*. These latter must also be either horizontal or vertical. Thus all changes in size always proceed on lines which are parallel either to CF/CB or to the Bust/Chest/Back lines of the draft.

When a scaffolding of grading lines has been prepared the pattern can be increased and decreased correctly to the next size or to more than one size. The various points of the pattern will retain their correct position *in relation to each other*, and consequently the basic structure of the pattern is preserved through all the changes of size.

Thus Fig. 2 shows an example of the way one size can be increased or decreased by the use of a scaffolding of grading lines, but no metric measurements are given for any method of grading in this edition of this book because, as has already been stated, every wholesale manufacturer will have his own method, which will involve fine calculations in millimetres and which will be worked out to suit a particular production method.

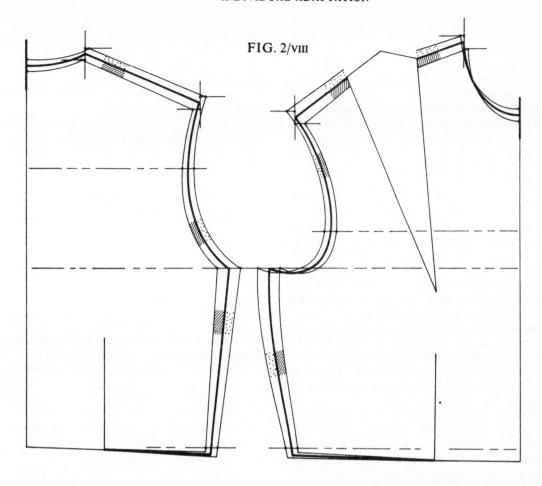

FIG. 2/VIII

INDIVIDUAL ADAPTATION

In adapting patterns to individual measurements the problem is somewhat different. Here, first of all, it is necessary to decide on a **suitable method of work for each pattern** so that more planning is involved and greater exercise of judgement is required in assessing the possibilities of a block pattern in relation to the changes that will have to be made on it. Since measurements vary, the work is always different for each person; but on the other hand, there is less responsibility for the final result as fitting and correcting are usually possible. Each adaptation is thus an individual operation, akin to individual pattern drafting, but quicker.

As there are many different ways or arriving at a correct result and no single precise method can be given (as is possible in grading), one can only explain this type of work on a variety of practical examples. These examples must cover a range of figure types expressed in measurements; or, to put it differently, the examples are **sets of measurements** which to every experienced cutter or fitter would **represent definite types of figure**. On such examples

one can show how a suitable block can best be adapted to each set, i.e. to each individual figure.

Naturally quite a big range of such 'figures' is possible, as there is considerable variety in measurement combinations. Nevertheless, a comparatively small number is sufficient to illustrate *the most usual* methods used, and to explain in a general way how to set about this work: practice soon develops the skill of seeing at a glance the changes required in a pattern and of making these changes in the best way and with the utmost economy of time.

Before giving the several examples demonstrating the most usual and practical adaptation methods, one other important point must be mentioned: patterns for individual figures can be adapted not only to their correct **measurements**, but also to their **shape of figure**, thus foreseeing at least some of the adjustments which a fitting would require. This, of course, is a matter of demanding greater understanding and experience of fitting problems than a mere adjustment of size. However, most dressmakers and tailors of experience aim at achieving this in order to save time on expensive fittings and corrections. Well taken measurements can mean a lot more to a cutter than just a correct size: they can actually show, at least to a certain extent, what the figure is like, i.e. its **shape and posture**, which, as has been shown throughout the earlier chapters, are **the two most important factors in fitting**.

To give a few examples: on an average figure the Chest measurement* (as taken according to this system—see note across the page), would be expected to be a little bigger than the x **Back measurement**, or at least equal.

When the back is wider than the chest, it usually indicates a round-shouldered figure with a more or less *stooping posture*, for which an experienced cutter/fitter would probably make suitable provision in the pattern, or at least allow good turnings and inlays where necessary. Sometimes, however, this may indicate a very muscular back, with heavy, square shoulders: here only personal observation at the measuring stage would help to confirm the shape of the figure, as the two types look, of course, very different and are easily distinguishable.

A **Bust measurement** which is equal to or larger than the **Hip measurement** usually indicates a figure with a prominent, i.e. high bust, and often *an erect posture*, particularly when this appears to be confirmed by a chest measure wider than normal. Various precautions can be taken in this direction when cutting out.

An **extra wide Back and Chest** measurement in proportion to the bust, usually means a 'flat' figure, possibly quite tall (if also long waisted). Difficulties may be expected in the armhole part which will probably work out *too narrow* (see armhole defects, Chapter Three). Sometimes side seam position may be wrong.

All this would probably be already a matter of **practical observation while taking the measurements**, when some 'coding' system can be used to record special remarks on the figure and its peculiarities. Measuring should confirm and check what one sees. However, it is particularly in cases where cutters do not take the measurements themselves that a study of these helps them to visualize the figure, always provided their measurements are reliable and have been taken in a specially agreed way.

In the first instance, therefore, **a set of measurements should be analyzed** in order to get some idea of the figure one is dealing with. This may suggest **a plan of work**, e.g. the most suitable block to use.

*The chest measurement referred to here is of course a measurement taken according to the instructions given in this method of cutting, i.e. fairly low down the chest (12–13 cm down CF) with shoulders held back, so as to obtain a maximum measurement which would allow for *chest ease* and 'sleeve pull'. In most Trade Patterns it is a measurement taken higher up the chest and so it works out smaller, in fact with the Chest measurement slightly narrower than x Back. This must be allowed for in any reference to the Chest made throughout the book.

EXAMPLE I

The middle column is the set of **individual measurements** to which the pattern is to be adapted (in other cases it is the left column). **The stock size blocks** shown on the right and left are the most suitable blocks for the adaptation, and one of them will be selected to be outlined and used according to the methods described below.

N.B. The letter 'C' means that the measurement is **correct** as it stands if the block in question is compared with the individual measurements.

Analysis

The set of individual measurements (middle column) represents a good average figure with nothing to indicate any special shape or posture problem of fit. In fact, the only problem here is to select the more suitable block of the two possible ones—the later—the 92 cm—shown on the right, or the smaller—the 88 cm—on the left.

EXAMPLE I

88 cm block		Individual measurements		92 cm block
B 88		B 91		B 92
H 94		H 96		H 98
W 68		W 66		W 70
LW 40/41	– C –	LW 40		LW 40/42
xB 35/36		xB 37	– C –	xB 36/37
Ch 37	– C –	Ch 37		Ch 38
Sh 12	– C –	Sh 12		Sh 12·5
TA 29	– C –	TA 29		TA 31

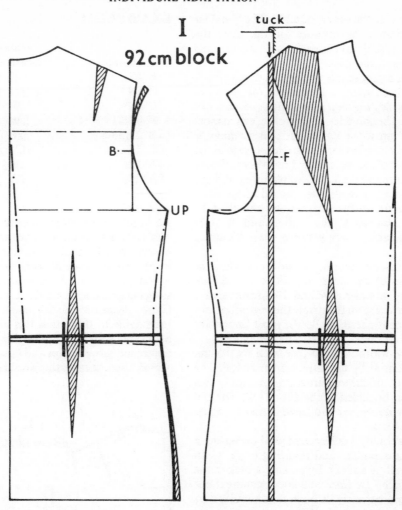

I
92 cm block

tuck

B·

·F

UP

FIG. 3/VIII

By comparing the measurements and considering the necessary alterations, it will appear at first glance that there is less to correct if the 88 cm block is used (the letter 'C' appears 4 times). However, on further consideration, and particularly bearing in mind the actual **methods to be used**, it will be found that the 92 cm block is equally convenient, and possibly even easier to use, mainly because reducing is generally easier and quicker than increasing.

Trace off the 92 cm block and note that **the x Back** is correct for the new set of measurements: therefore *no change* can be made at the back UP either, and *the Bust width* will have to be reduced entirely on the front (Fig. 3).

Bust and chest (half pattern), as well as shoulder, must all lose and this can be done by making a 0·5 cm deep tuck through the whole length of the Front, losing, of course, some hip width as well out of the required hip reduction. The tuck must be kept the *same width right through* and it is advisable to crease the paper first at right angles to the

Bust line or by folding the lower edge—if horizontal—back over itself, then measuring the full width of the tuck *from the crease* in several places, and finally folding it out.

Thus using a tuck through the front loses width in four (or even five) places *in one operation*. It now remains to reduce **the Hip measurement** by a further amount that will make it 1 cm less on the half pattern. First of all the **back hip width** must be checked to see that it corresponds to the **usual drafting proportion** of $\frac{1}{4}$ Hip measurement, in this case approximately 24 cm for a 96 cm Hip measurement. Anything over and above this should be lost on the back side seam at hip level.

The remaining measurements require only very simple adjustments: the **back shoulder** is shortened by 0·5 cm, **the LW** is raised to make it correct. The **waist width** has already been reduced by the tuck: it can be further reduced by increasing slightly the waist darts, or *left as it is until the fitting*.

The armhole can be used as it is (TA + 12–13 cm) taking

care to check later that the sleeve matches. **The Shoulder dart** can be considered as suitable for the size: the shoulderblade dart is seldom changed, except for a *special fit* (e.g. for very round shoulders).

Altogether this is a very simple and quick adaptation. It will already have been noted that *some of the measurements can be left as they are until after a fitting*, even if not absolutely correct. The shoulder, for instance, can in most cases be ignored, provided its length *plus turnings* is considered sufficient to allow for a possible increase at the fitting. The position of the waistline, if not very different (not more than 1 cm) and if no *detailed* planning of darts is required by the style, can also be ignored at the early stage. All this speeds up the adaptation, but must be remembered and *checked* at the fitting, and suitable turnings made available, *where necessary*, when cutting out.

If, for the sake of comparison, one now considers **the adaptation from an 88 cm block**, it will be found that although the chest, shoulder, LW and TA (armhole) are as on the block, these are on the whole the less important measurements (except chest), while the most important ones—bust, hips and xBack—have to be increased.

Since the x Back width must be increased by 0·5 cm, this means increasing it by the same 0·5 cm at UP. The remaining 1 cm out of the required 1·5 cm bust width addition must then be added at the Front UP. The hip width in the back will have to be adjusted to make it equal a quarter of 96 = 24 cm.

N.B. There are actually **4 different ways of increasing a pattern**: by cutting a pattern and inserting extra width (the opposite of making a tuck); by making a tuck in the paper *before tracing off the block* and later opening it out (tuck must be placed correctly through the shoulder); by adding the extra width down the CB and then reducing the neckline; or simply by adding the width down the side (grading method) and then reshaping the side seam and, if necessary, the armhole. Whichever method of increasing is chosen—it will generally be slower than 'reducing'.

In this example, *when using the 88 cm block*, the remaining bust width increase (1 cm) must be made on the front at UP, adding also 0·5 cm to the hip width: the side seam will then be re-drawn between these new points (as in Fig. 4) after first joining them by *a straight line*, and will not be parallel to the original seam. The Shoulder dart must be increased to 7 cm and because of this the shoulder, which was *originally correct*, will have to be lengthened to make up for the bigger dart. The chest width (also originally correct) may have to be slightly widened for the same reason (dart increase).

Thus the whole adaptation from the 88 cm block proves to be more complicated than from a 92 cm block and would take more time. It is therefore well worth giving a few minutes to a careful analysis of the measurements before starting on an adaptation, and with some practice this becomes a matter of routine.

EXAMPLE II

88 cm block		Individual measurements		92 cm block
B 88		B 84		B 92
H 94		H 93		H 98
W 68		W 64		W 70
LW 40/41	– C –	LW 41		LW 40/42
xB 35/36		xB 37		xB 36/37
Ch 37		Ch 36		Ch 38
Sh 12		Sh 12·5	– C –	Sh 12·5
TA 29		TA 28		TA 31

Analysis

As hardly any measurements are correct (C) in either block, it is natural to assume that the smaller block will be nearer to the required size. In both cases **the x Back width**—so often the **deciding factor**—has to be increased, which points to a somewhat unusual figure, in fact a **stooping posture**, the x Back being 1 cm wider than the Chest (because of the small bust it would not be reasonable to think that this is a figure with a muscular back and shoulders). The fairly long LW and the big difference between hips and bust support this assumption.

N.B. In most cases this would of course be confirmed by

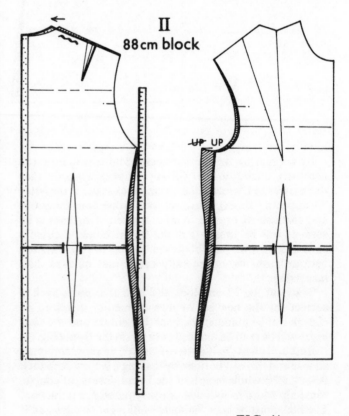

II
88 cm block

FIG. 4/VIII

personal observation when taking measurements.

Even before outlining the **88 cm block** consider the **xB width** since the bust cannot be adjusted correctly until this has been dealt with, and also because it may suggest a plan of work. One cm can be added to the back through a tuck made beforehand in the paper, or simply down the CB, *before outlining the block* (Fig. 4). In the latter case the NP can be *moved back* the full amount, as a neckline of an 88 cm block should be sufficient for size. One could even leave it a little wider to allow more *back neckline fullness*, if it is considered suitable for this type of figure (for prominent shoulder blades, for example). Such a 'fitting' adjustment may not necessarily be attempted by a beginner, but it should at least be considered as a likely correction at the fitting: therefore a *bigger turning* than usual should be allowed at the end of the back shoulder, particularly as *the shoulderblade dart* may also need increasing slightly to clear the armhole. The 1 cm CB addition, which must always be *parallel to CB*, never sloping in or out, will of course increase the hip width unnecessarily and this surplus width and a little more will have to come off the side seam to make the back hip width, as usual, equal to a quarter of the Hip measurement: in this case it is a quarter of 93 = 23. The front hip width is always 3 cm bigger than the back, so 26 cm plus is measured from CF for the new HP, actually only just inside the original line.

Since **the bust width** was increased by 1 cm in the back *because of the wider xB measurement*, the front will have to be reduced more at UP. Measure the bust width of the back, i.e. CB to UP = 23·5 cm and deduct this from *the required total bust width*, i.e. $\frac{1}{2}B + 5$ cm $= \frac{84}{2} + 5 = 47$. The result will be 23·5 cm for the front. Measure this from CF and mark the new UP.

N.B. Note that back and front width now work out the same, which is very typical for a stooping and/or flat-chested figure.

Join new front UP and HP, first by a *straight line* (as in drafting), from which the correct curving of the side seam can be done in the usual way, i.e. by going in 1 cm at the waist. The latter may be dropped 0·5 cm or considered as correct *until the fitting*.

The Chest being only 0·5 cm narrower, it is simplest to reduce it by *moving the chest point 0·5 cm in* and then reshaping the armhole, hollowing it out more. Alternatively, the chest width could be ignored until the fitting, though the big loss of width on the *front armhole* will in any case make the hollowing out necessary.

N.B. If the figure had **a 36 cm xBack**, there would have been some advantage in using the 92 cm block, and taking out a tuck through the front (later lengthening shoulder). The side seam would then be re-drawn completely, after further reductions at UP and HP. In any case if an 88 cm block were not available, a 92 cm block would be a possible alternative, although the adjustments would be different.

EXAMPLE III

Individual measurements		92 cm block
B 97		B 92
H 99		H 98
W 68		W 70
LW 38		LW 40/42
xB 36	– C –	xB 36
Ch 40		Ch 38
Sh 12		Sh 12·5
TA 29		TA 31

Analysis

The measurements indicate a figure which probably has an erect posture, a straight, short back, narrow for the size, and a prominent bust. The bigger than usual difference between x Back and Chest, and the smaller one between Bust (97) and Hips (99) tends to support this assumption. With only the bust considerably bigger (i.e. a 'full bust' figure), and all other measurements very close to the 92 cm average pattern, this is obviously the best block to use.

As the xB is correct (36 cm), the back of the block can be used almost as it is. No bust width addition is of course possible at back UP, only a small addition at HP: this, for the total **hip increase** of 1 cm, works out a quarter of this for the back and the same for the front.

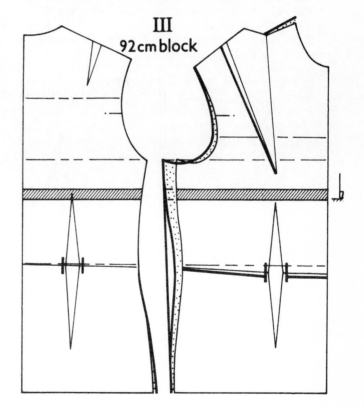

FIG. 5/VIII

A big change is the **shortening of the LW** by 3–4 cm. When the amount by which it is to be shortened is 1 cm or more, it is best to make **a horizontal tuck across**, somewhere halfway between armhole and waist, as shown in Fig. 5.

The Bust width addition must be made entirely on the front and as it is considerable (2·5 cm), *the side seam* will have to be *reshaped*. **The Chest** needs 1 cm extra width; since neither hips nor chest require this increase, it is simpler to add the 1 cm at chest level only, and to re-shape the armhole accordingly.

It is advisable to make the **Shoulder dart** bigger (8 cm) and this will make the shoulder 0·5 cm shorter—as required. A figure with a prominent bust is quite likely to need an even deeper dart at the fitting—allow for this when cutting out.

The *waist width* has been increased a little by the re-shaping of the side seam. It can easily be tightened by making the Waist darts deeper, possibly at the fitting.

EXAMPLE IV

Individual measurements		108 cm block
B 109		B 108
H 112		H 114
W 83		W 84/86
LW 40		LW 42/44
xB 42		xB 40/41
Ch 43	– C –	Ch 43
Sh 12·5		Sh 13·5
TA 37·5		TA 36/37

Analysis

The measurements indicate a fairly large, short-waisted figure with a broad back. With little difference between back and chest, and between bust and hips, it is likely to be a rather 'stocky' figure with heavy shoulders. This is confirmed by the big Top Arm measurement.

It is not a difficult adaptation, particularly if a 108 cm block is available, though a 112 cm block could also be used.

Increase **the xB** by 1 cm either by inserting this width through the shoulder, adding down CB or simply by adding it at the armhole and UP, without, however, increasing the length of the shoulder. If widened right through or at CB (which is often quickest), hips and shoulder will need reducing more.

For shortening **the waist length** use a horizontal tuck as in the previous example. **The shoulder** is rather short in proportion to the xB and Ch measurements: it is therefore probably square (high). Shorten it to the required length, or leave until the fitting.

N.B. When shortening or lengthening the shoulder by over 1 cm it may sometimes be necessary *to consider its slant*, otherwise cutting off at the end may loosen it too much (and vice versa). To retain the original shoulder slant of the block a 'grading' method must be used. In this case, however, for this type of figure any loosening would probably not be a disadvantage as the shoulder may even have to be let out at the fitting (Fig. 6—dot-dash line).

The hips, 2 cm smaller than the block, must lose 0·5 cm on each seam unless the back was widened *right through*,

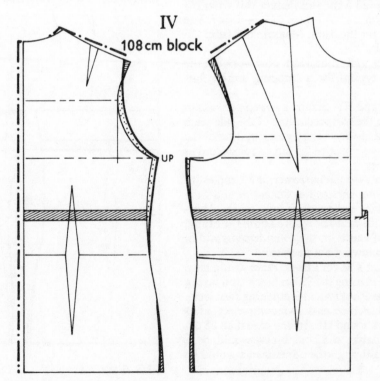

IV

108 cm block

FIG. 6/VIII

in which case the loss at the seam *in the back* will be 0·5 cm plus the additional 1 cm = 1·5 cm.

The **shoulder dart** can be left as it is. **The armhole** should not present a problem because there is every reason to think that in this case an increase may be made *upwards*, i.e. by letting out at SP because of a possible squaring of shoulders. **N.B.** Larger figures often need armholes equal to Top Arm +15 cm.

The **waist width** can be considered as correct, unless it became too loose when it was widened right through. In this case, because of the shape of the figure, it may even be possible to tighten it **at the side seam** (test at fitting).

EXAMPLE V

Individual measurements		108 cm block
B 106		B 108
H 120		H 114
LW 42	– C –	LW 42/44
xB 42		xB 40/41
Ch 41		Ch 43
Sh 15		Sh 13·5
TA 37	– C –	TA 36/37

Analysis

This is a different type of figure, expanding towards the hips which are 14 cm bigger than the bust ('pear-shaped'). The waist is also bigger than average for the size of the bust (probably prominent abdomen). When measuring, it is not always easy to get the exact *position of the waist*, or

even length of shoulder, and in fact the person fitted will sometimes herself indicate where she likes her 'waist' to be. To a certain extent this difficulty may apply also to the xBack and Chest. Some of the measurements, therefore, may be noted down in a less definite way.

The main adjustment here is the increase of hip width— a total of 6 cm more than the block—which gives 1·5 cm to add on back and on front. Before doing this, however 0·5 cm **extra xB** should be added down CB and the neckline then reduced, this increasing **the length of shoulder** at NP, before lengthening it further at SP (see Fig. 7).

The reduction of the bust width has to be made on the front only, i.e. the whole 1 cm plus the 0·5 cm *just added in the back* (1·5 cm) is taken off at the front UP.

N.B. This *unnecessary* increase of bust width in the back (0·5 cm) cannot be avoided as it usually places the underarm seam more correctly on the figure in relation to the person's width of back.

It now remains to increase **the hip width** and since the back has already been widened by 0·5 cm (on CB) only another 1 cm is added at back HP and 1·5 cm at the front HP. In the back the *small* hip addition can run into the seam; but in the front, because of the 1·5 cm loss at bust level, *the slope of the seam alters too much*, and it is necessary to re-draw the whole seam.

The waist must be measured to include any additions (at CB and side seams) and then *re-planned for the bigger size*—45 cm instead of 43 cm—reducing, i.e. letting out the darts if necessary.

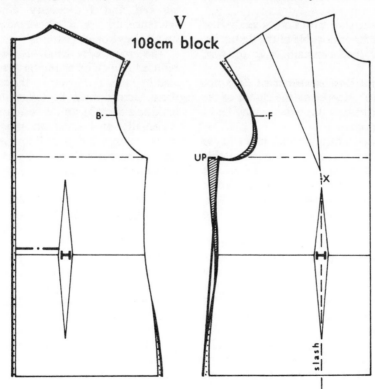

V
108cm block

FIG. 7/VIII

If the shape of the figure, observed at the measuring stage, is taken into consideration (prominent abdomen? prominent seat?) it may be an advantage to allow the extra hip width required down the front and/or down CB instead of in the side seams. This, according to the defect, would mean either transferring a little of the shoulder dart into the hem or making a simple *sloping-out* (say 1 cm) addition at CB (see Shape of Figure defects—Chapter Two).

The five examples given are sufficient to demonstrate the practical methods from which a few simple rules can be deduced for individual pattern adaptation.

It is obvious from these examples that a few **stock size blocks** can be adapted to **cover a big range of individual sizes**. The three blocks used here would be sufficient for most purposes, possibly with yet another, bigger size (e.g. B 116 cm) where many large figures have to be provided for.

The other important thing to realize is that in order to adapt an average block correctly and quickly to fit an individual figure, one must know the construction of the block in all its details, remembering all its **basic proportions** such as back hip width being always equal to a quarter of the Hip measurement; front hips—always 3 cm wider; Bust width in the back (CB-UP) always 5·5 cm (6–7 cm) more than x Back measurement, etc. In fact one must know the draft well and keep all these figures in one's head while working on the pattern. **N.B.** The best plan is to have all the measurements of the block clearly written on it, as well as some of the basic proportions.

It is generally advisable to start with a quick **analysis of the measurements**, and as far as possible of the figure, i.e. try to visualize it. After that a certain *order of work* usually suggests itself.

It will be noted that **the Bust measurement** does not necessarily have a decisive influence on the choice of the block: other factors, particularly the xBack, may be of equal, if not greater importance.

The xB measurement often indicates which block to use and is also generally the best clue as to the most suitable method of adaptation. The chest measurement does not have this effect and can sometimes even be disregarded or simply taken 'in proportion' to the xBack, i.e. 1·5–2·5 cm bigger, provided one is certain that it is *not unusually big* and that it can be checked at a fitting.

As was seen from the various examples, **some measurements are more important than others** and so have to be considered more carefully. Chest, shoulder, waist width and armhole—except when *unusual* for the size of the figure—are less important and decisive for the correct fit of the pattern and can in many cases be left to the fitting. The Bust, Hip, x Back and usually the LW (indicating height of figure) should always be adjusted on the new pattern (though a 0·5–1 cm difference in LW can be ignored until the fitting). However, often a less important

measurement is actually a good indicator of the *type of figure* one is dealing with. It is therefore advisable always to take the full set of these basic measurements plus, of course, any other which might be useful for the details of the style (a 'lowered' waist, a depth of yoke etc.).

When outlining the block (back and front can be done quite separately), leave paper outside where additions are likely to be needed, otherwise pasting will be necessary. With regard to the various methods of adding or reducing, it was seen that there are actually **four ways of increasing the pattern**. There are, however, only **three practical ways of reducing**, and of these taking off width down CB and particularly CF is not always suitable.

The armhole of an adapted pattern may occasionally present a problem, but generally it is easily checked and adjusted at the fitting. It should, however, be always **carefully measured after the adaptation** (holding tape measure on edge) to get a clear idea of the situation, i.e. to see if it is nearly correct (within 1 cm or so), or too large, or too small. If too large, it is advisable to reduce it straight away by raising UP, or at least to leave a good turning here for the fitting.

SLEEVE ADAPTATION

The sleeve, though originally based on the Top Arm measurement, **must nevertheless fit the correct armhole**, i.e. the armhole considered suitable for the figure. Its crown edge should therefore always be a little longer (at least 1·5–2 cm) than the *final* armhole size, and this *must be checked*, and if necessary, adjusted. **N.B.** For quick reference, it is useful to have *the crown edge length* written on all sleeve block patterns.

The crown edge length is changed, i.e. increased or reduced *mainly* by changing the width of the sleeve, but also by raising or lowering the crown at the fitting. Both these factors must be taken into consideration when making a decision on sleeve adaptation. The sleeve width is usually at least 5 cm more than the Top Arm measurement, but may be more, not only for various types of garments (e.g. coats) or different styles, but also for some *shapes* of arm and armhole (e.g. for some large figures).

To increase the sleeve width for an individual adaptation e.g. by 1·5 cm, the width is added—as in grading—half through the middle and the rest equally on both edges. For bigger sizes 3 mm **extra height** must be added at the top (at point T) for every 1+ cm more of top arm measurement; but the crown may be left as it is, i.e. *average*, when *reducing* the sleeve block to a smaller size.

If the sleeve is **widened entirely on the seam edges** (to avoid having to *insert* extra width through the middle or making tucks in paper before outlining), then the sleeve must later be re-folded lengthwise into *4 equal sections* to obtain the correct new position for the Back Line and the Forearm, i.e. to find points B and F.

SKIRT ADAPTATION

Skirts are very easy to adapt and the size, i.e. **the hip width** can be quickly changed by reducing or increasing the pattern down the CD and CF lines. This can even be done before outlining the block. The **waist width**, however, i.e. **the darts**, have to be adjusted individually according to the required waist measurement.

To increase the size by 2 cm (e.g. from 98 cm to 100 cm measurement) add 0·5 cm all the way down CF and 0·5 cm down CB. Place the block pattern with its CF edge 0·5 cm from the right edge of the paper, outline it and, before cutting out, add 0·5 cm to the CB, keeping the new line absolutely parallel to the edge of the block. The width of *the half-pattern* is thus increased by 1 cm (2 cm total increase) right through without any change in the 'line' of the skirt.

To reduce the size by 2 cm, take 0·5 cm off the CF by placing the block so that it projects 0·5 cm beyond the right edge of the paper; then outline and lose 0·5 cm all the way down the CB. It is, in fact, quite convenient to have for this purpose a skirt block with several parallel lines drawn *inside* the CF and CB at 0·5 cm distance from each other.

The adaptation will in each case change the waist, though not necessarily as required by the new measurements, so that the darts must always be checked and increased, decreased or even re-arranged for the individual figure.

FITTING ADJUSTMENTS IN ADAPTATIONS

Any **fitting adjustments**, such as a change in the balance or shoulder slant of a bodice, which can be introduced into an individual pattern *while adapting it*, would of course depend entirely on one's experience and ability to *visualize the shape of the figure clearly*. For beginners it is best not to attempt it so as not to endanger the result of the whole operation of adapting a block to a new set of measurements. With more practice in fitting and increased confidence it will happen quite naturally that certain details will be added to change *the fit* as well as *the size* of the pattern, thus speeding up, simplifying and reducing the number of fittings which, of course, is the aim of every experienced and skilled fitter.

ABBREVIATIONS AND REFERENCE LETTERS

CB	Centre Back
CF	Centre Front
NW	Natural Waist level
NP	Neck Point
SP	Shoulder Point
UP	Underarm Point
HP	Hip Point
WP	Waist Point
HW	Hip Width, i.e. Hip measurement +6 cm
WR	Waist Reduction
B	Bust measurement
H	Hip measurement
W	Waist measurement (or Waist point)
LW	Length to Waist measurement (down CB)
xB	Back measurement (across back)
Ch	Chest measurement (approx. 12 cm down CF)
Sh	Shoulder length

In Sleeve Patterns

TA	Top Arm measurement
DC	Depth of Crown
B	Back Inset point (or top of Back line)
F	Front Inset point (or top of Forearm)
T	highest point of sleeve crown (of top line)
U	lowest point of crown (Top of Underarm line)
E	Elbow point or Elbow level

Various other abbreviations:

SG	Straight Grain
L-SG	Lengthwise (or selvedge) Straight grain
X-SG	Crosswise Straight Grain
Point X	Highest point of Bust
Point G	Gusset point
SP-U	Kimono armhole
U-G	Kimono gusset line
OX	Depth of Crutch (in slacks)

TABLE OF AVERAGE MEASUREMENTS AND PROPORTIONS

MEASUREMENTS

PROPORTIONS

	Bust B	Hips H	Waist W	Waist Length LW	xBack xB	Chest Ch	Shoulder SH	Top Arm TA	Depth of armhole (*Bust line*) Back UP	Point O CB	Back neck width	Depth of armhole (*Bust line*)	Back UP	Dart	Armhole (*approx.*)
I	80+10	86+6	64	38/40(36)	33/34	35	12−	28		2	6·5 −	20·5	5	6	40
II	84	90	66	39/41	34/35	36	12	29		2·5	6·5	20·5+	5	6·5	41
III	88	94	68	39·5/41·5	35/36	37	12·5−	30		3	7 −	21	5	7	42
IV	92	98	70	40/42	36/37	38	12·5	31		3	7	21·5	5·5	7·5	43
V	96	102	72	40·5/42·5	37/38	39	13−	32		3·5	7·5 −	22	6	8	44·5
VI	100	106	76	41/43	38/39	40	13	33		3·5	7·5	22·5	6	8·5	46
VII	104	110	80	41·5/43·5	39/40	42	13·5	34·5		4	8 −	23	6·5	9	47
VIII	108	114	84/86	42/44	40/41	43	13·5	36/37		4	8	23·5	7	9·5	48
IX	112	118	88/90	42·5/44	41/42	44·5	14	38		4·5	8·5 −	24	7	10	50
X	116	122	92	43/45	42/43	46	14·5	39/40		4·5	8·5	24·5	7	10·5	51/52

LENGTH TO WAIST: the shorter LW is based on an average height of 160–165 cm (5′4″–5′5″); the longer is for taller figures. LW is not dependent on or connected with the other measurements, except height, and a shorter or longer waist can occur in any 'Size'. The LW can, therefore, be always increased without affecting the other proportions of the draft.

xBACK WIDTH: a slightly wider xBack can be used in each case. This is particularly useful in the *smaller sizes* where back width often does not conform to a strictly graded' scale. The *small* addition can be made without any change in the draft, e.g. without changing the position of UP (though shoulder may have to be lengthened).

INDEX